D0753829

Essential Touch

Meeting the Needs of Young Children

Frances M. Carlson

National Association for the Education of Young Children
Washington, DC

Permissions:
Lyrics to "Human Touch" by Bruce Springsteen. Copyright © 1992 Bruce Springsteen. Reprinted by permission. International copyright secured. All rights reserved.

Photographs copyrights © by: Frances M. Carlson *38, 54, 56, 94, back cover*; Cleo Freelance Photography *18*; Kathy Henson *iii*; Jean-Claude Lejeune *104*; Marilyn Nolt *viii, 4, 78*; Ellen B. Senisi *front cover*; Christina Tolomei *16*. All rights reserved.

National Association for the Education of Young Children
1313 L Street NW, Suite 500
Washington, DC 20005-4101
202-232-8777 or 800-424-2460
www.naeyc.org

Through its publications program the National Association for the Education of Young Children (NAEYC) provides a forum for discussion of major issues and ideas in the early childhood field, with the hope of provoking thought and promoting professional growth. The views expressed or implied in this book are not necessarily those of the Association.

Carol Copple, *publications director*. Bry Pollack, *senior editor*. Malini Dominey, *design and production*. Lisa Bowles, *editorial associate*. Natalie Klein Cavanagh, *photo editor and editorial assistance*. Mary Gawlik, *editorial assistance*.

Library of Congress Control Number: 2006931810
ISBN 978-1-928896-40-1
NAEYC Item #799

For my sister, Nancy,
who made everything better with a hug.
I miss you.

About the Author

Frances M. Carlson has administered child development programs for the Department of the Army, the Internal Revenue Service, Wachovia Bank, Sheltering Arms, and Turner Broadcasting Systems. She currently works as an early childhood care and education instructor at Chattahoochee Technical College in Dallas, Georgia.

Frances serves as a Child Development Associate (CDA) adviser, a mentor director for other early childhood program directors, and the faculty adviser for her college's student group—Chattahoochee Technical College Association on Young Children. For NAEYC, she is a consulting editor and cofacilitator for its Men in Education Network (MEN) Interest Forum.

Frances has a master's degree in early childhood education from Concordia University in St. Paul, Minnesota. She is also a certified first aid and CPR instructor for the American Heart Association. In her free time, she enjoys riding roller coasters with her three children, Adam, Sam, and Caty.

"Where touching begins, there love and humanity also begin."

—Ashley Montagu,
Touching: The Human Significance of the Skin

"Tell me, in a world without pity
Do you think what I'm askin's too much
I just want something to hold on to
And a little of that human touch."

—Bruce Springsteen,
"Human Touch"

Contents

Acknowledgments

To my family—thank you for being my safe place.

Thanks to Lynn Gehrke, Concordia University–St. Paul; Carol Plummer, Louisiana State University; Jane Lannak, Boston University; Sarah Farquhar, ChildForum Research Network–New Zealand; Linda Storm, Infant Massage USA; and Bryan G. Nelson, MenTeach, for being passionate about this topic and for wanting more information on it to be available.

Special thanks to the Early Childhood Care & Education students at Chattahoochee Technical College for your willingness to discuss this topic and share your stories with me. Your dedication to improving children's lives inspires me every day and made writing this book possible. To Carol Copple and Bry Pollack—thanks for your kindness, patience, and reassurance from beginning to end.

Last of all, my most special thanks to Don Piburn, for sharing my zeal for returning touch to young children's lives and for reading, editing, and believing in this work and its importance. I couldn't have done it without you, Don. E ku'u hoaaloha, mahalo nui loa!

About This Book

Acknowledging my own comfort level with touch has been a critical factor in my relationships with others because I am not a "touchy-feely" person. Yet when I think of the times in my life when I felt most comforted and most loved, those moments involved touch. Some of those times were when I was 4 years old and curled up in a blanket on my mama's lap, when a nurse named Ruby held my hand continuously during an intense labor with my third child, and when a colleague hugged me without saying a word when he heard my sister had died. Touch communicates as nothing else can, and it is irreplaceable in our lives and in our classrooms. It is that idea that motivates me as an early childhood educator, and it was the primary motivation for my writing this book.

Chapter One introduces the concepts of touch and sets the context for later chapters. **Chapter Two** examines the many, powerful ways that touch and touch experiences affect young children physically, cognitively, socially, and emotionally, as well as the therapeutic benefits of human touch. **Chapter Three** paints a picture of a developmentally appropriate early childhood program where touch is a critical pedagogical element. A "touch curriculum" is outlined in **Chapter Four,** describing what children should learn about body awareness, healthy sexuality, and body ownership as infants, toddlers, and preschoolers. Policies and programs that can safeguard both children from sexual abuse and caregivers from allegations of inappropriate touching are addressed in **Chapter Five.** And finally, **Chapter Six** focuses on children with touch-related special needs. The **References** and **Resources** sections offer lists of books on touch for educators and for young children, as well as some useful Web sites. Additional practical resources for educators, such as sample staff and family handbook policies, are provided in the **Appendixes.**

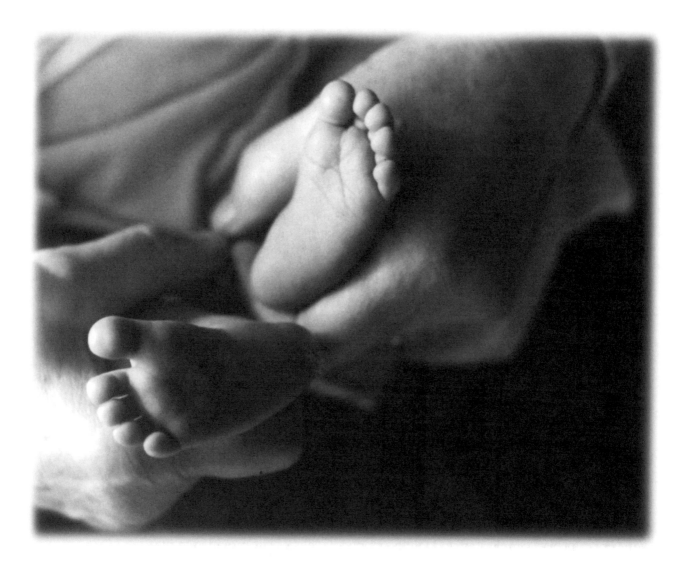

Chapter 1

Taking a Look at Touch

The uterine contractions of labor constitute the beginning caressing of the baby. (Montagu 1986:68)

So important is the role of touch that our lives begin with it. Its importance continues into early childhood, as one of the primary senses through which preverbal infants and toddlers relate to the world, and it continues to play a role in older children's development and learning. In the early childhood setting, touch is about *physical contact* between children and their caregivers and peers, and about providing young children with *tactile experiences* of the world around them. Both kinds of touch are absolutely essential. So it is critical that those who work in settings where children spend so much time meet their needs for touch, and in ways that are educational, appropriate, respectful, and nurturing.

Creating a learning environment rich with opportunities to experience and experiment with tactile sensations is something most teachers of young children are comfortable with and do routinely in their programs. Children feel objects of different shapes and textures; they push, pull, lift, squeeze, and toss things; they put their hands in water and sand. It's the other kind of touch where things get complicated.

> For the past 20 years, the trend toward abstaining from touch in schools has been growing in direct response to the growth in sensitivity toward the problems of sexual harassment, molestation, and abuse. In an effort to keep one step ahead of sexual offenders, more and more schools are sending the message to adults—hands off! . . . Touching children in schools has become virtually taboo. (Del Prete 1997: 59)

Many early childhood educators are confused and ambivalent about the touch connection with children. They hate the idea of babies, toddlers, and preschoolers, especially, spending their days without the nurture and stimulation of human contact. Yet they worry about how to protect the children and themselves in a climate of concern about abuse. Living in a relatively "low-touch" culture, many Americans have found minimal-touch and no-touch policies more palatable than might be the case in a country where continuous skin-to-skin contact between young children and their caregivers is the norm from birth (Small 1998). And the belief that somehow too much touch will spoil a child also keeps young children from receiving sufficient physical contact.

But when it comes to how much and what types of physical contact belong in early childhood programs, research and practical wisdom offer a clear answer: Young children need positive human touch, and lots of it, in all its forms—carrying, swinging, rolling, holding, a backrub, a hug, a pat, a high-five, rough-and-tumble play, even massage. Nurturing touch from their caregivers is essential for children to feel loved and secure; interactions with their peers help develop social and emotional competence.

Essential Touch

Moreover, teachers must understand that withholding touch can be just as physically and emotionally harmful to a child as sexual abuse or physical abuse such as hitting, grabbing, spanking, and shaking. When children of any age are denied touch or when they experience it only in the context of aggression or punishment, they are deprived of the nurturing environment they need to thrive and grow. They also will lack experiences to prepare them to discern touch that is loving and appropriate from touch that is dangerous and inappropriate—and thus they are more vulnerable to sexual exploitation.

Early childhood teachers and directors very much want to create nurturing environments for children and are eager to receive guidance and support to help them do so. This book is for them and the children they care for.

Chapter 2

The Importance of Touch in Development and Learning

One day when my toddler son and I were walking around at the nature preserve he noticed two geese. He walked up to one and began to pat it on the head. When the goose turned, my son *quickly* ran back to me, grabbing hold of my leg. After a minute or two, he let go and walked back to the goose. I have a picture of him standing there, eye-to-eye with the goose, patting it contentedly on the head.

   —A mother reflecting on the role of touch in attachment

Since ancient times, touch has been recognized as playing a role in health. Therapeutic touch was described by the Chinese in the first guide to acupuncture in 2760 BC. Around 400 BC, the Greek physician Hippocrates was teaching that rubbing the body led to optimum growth. These days we know much more about the fundamental role that tactile experiences, especially positive human touch, play in human development and learning. Skin-to-skin contact selectively stimulates and suppresses powerful chemicals in the brain, for example.

As a result, not only does touch play a pivotal and natural role in physical and cognitive development, it also can have significant therapeutic benefits. In the domains of emotional and social development, touch is critical in fostering bonding between children and their caregivers, as well as contributes to social and emotional competence.

In other words, touch is essential in every aspect of a young child's life.

Touch in physical and cognitive development

The physical benefits of touch begin as soon as we are born. Newborns who experience skin-to-skin contact with their mothers soon after birth cry less, sleep longer, and have longer periods of quiet alertness, which is when learning most often occurs. They also have higher blood sugar levels—a positive outcome in newborns—and better maintain their body temperature (Anderson et al. 2003). Skin-to-skin contact also is important for successful breastfeeding. If left undisturbed on the mother's stomach immediately following birth, newborns "exhibit a very specific sequence of movements— lip-smacking, then head-turning and salivating—that culminate in the newborn's crawling up to the breast on its own, locating the nipple, and starting to feed" (Johnson & Johnson 1995). When skin-to-skin contact is interrupted soon after birth, though—if the baby is removed for a bath or a bottle, for example—initiating or resuming breastfeeding becomes more difficult. Just 24 hours of skin-to-skin contact results in physical (and emotional) gains for the baby for months following birth (Ferber & Makhoul 2004).

Conversely, without adequate touch, infants may fail to thrive or may even die. An early documented instance of death from lack of touch occurred in the 13th century in a misguided experiment by Frederick II, the German king and emperor of the Holy Roman Empire. A curious and scientifically minded man, Frederick was attempting to discover what language young children would develop if they had no exposure to speech. He instructed that 50 newborns be taken from their mothers and given to caregivers who were not to speak or provide care other than feeding and bathing as necessary. But Frederick never got the answer to his question because, tragically, all the children died.

The same outcome was observed in landmark studies by pediatrician Henry Chapin around 1915 and psychiatrist René Spitz in the 1940s in institutional care environments. They too observed that infants who received adequate food and sanitation but no physical contact beyond that often failed to thrive or died. Because the children's physical needs were being met, the two researchers concluded that the missing essential factor was nurturing touch (see Montagu 1986). Now a recognized medical condition, "failure to thrive" describes children in settings lacking responsive and nurturing care who should be thriving in the absence of disease or physiological abnormalities but are not (Hockenberry, Wilson, & Winkelstein 2005). In such children, weight gain is slow or nonexistent, and intelligence test scores are lower than average (Holden 1996).

Touch as therapy

Mothers instinctively embrace their newborns, and science confirms the therapeutic benefits of that natural impulse. One therapeutic touch intervention originated in the late 1970s in the overcrowded neonatal units of Bogota, Colombia. Because incubators were in short supply, mothers of premature infants were given their babies to hold 24 hours a day. They tucked the infants under their clothing, like a baby kangaroo would be in its mother's pouch. Doctors studying the practice noticed that the babies thrived; mortality rates fell from the typical 70 percent to 30 percent. They, and later others elsewhere, began prescribing the practice, referred to as "kangaroo care." This touch technique involves having the naked (but diapered) newborn lie in an upright

Touch as Therapy for Maternal Depression

Depression in new mothers is not uncommon. As hazardous as it can be for the mother, the effects of maternal depression on her child are also dangerous, both physically and emotionally. Mothers with depression are less physically and emotionally available to their babies and usually provide them with less facial and tactile stimulation (Weller & Feldman 2003). When they look at their babies, their facial expressions tend to be flat and emotionless. Their babies mirror these expressions back, smiling and laughing less. They look at their mothers less often and have diminished responses to their mothers' faces (Cohn & Tronick 1989). When mothers with depression touch their infants, it usually is in negative ways such as poking and jabbing. This kind of touching is not physically or emotionally productive for the infant.

Teaching mothers with depression how to massage their infants can be healing for both mother and child. Through this intervention, the infant receives the benefits of positive touch from the mother, and the mother's depression often decreases (Field 2001). As the mother's mood improves, she becomes more physically and emotionally available to her baby. She begins to stimulate the baby more responsively, with both increased facial expressions and appropriate tactile interactions. She smiles more, touches in more caring ways, and is more engaged in her interactions with the baby. Thus, touch as a therapy for maternal depression benefits both mother and child.

position on the mother's (or father's) bare chest, with the baby's head turned so that his ear is directly over his parent's heart (Richardson 1997). As described above, the physical benefits of skin-to-skin contact such as kangaroo care are now well documented (Anderson et al. 2003; Ferber & Makhoul 2004).

Touch therapy in the form of massage also shows benefits in preterm infancy and beyond. Massaged infants experience fewer colds and fewer episodes of diarrhea than nonmassaged infants do (Field 2001). Preterm infants also gain more weight when massaged regularly (Field, Schanberg, & Scafidi 1986). In one study, preterm infants treated with Swedish (deep pressure) massage grew faster and gained more weight, and they were more alert and responsive than nonmassaged infants. The touch therapy also had financial advantages; the infants were discharged an average of six days early, saving some $3,000 per child (Field 2001). The type of massage seems to matter. Full-term infants massaged with moderate pressure gain more weight, grow faster, exhibit lower excitability and depression, and have less agitated sleep behavior compared with infants who receive light pressure touch (Field et al. 2004).

Massage has therapeutic benefits with later health conditions, too. Children who have suffered burns report less pain during treatment after they receive massage therapy, and children with cerebral palsy become less spastic and gain in muscle flexibility and in fine motor and gross motor control (Hernandez-Reif et al. 2005).

Touch in the form of massage also seems to have significant cognitive benefits. In one study, for example, preschoolers who were either read to or massaged prior to taking three perceptual-motor tests performed better after the 15-minute massage (Hart et al. 1998). The massage seemed particularly beneficial for the "high-strung" or "anxious" children. The researchers concluded that the massage was more effective than being read to in decreasing the children's anxiety, thus increasing their cognitive performance.

Touch as neurochemical trigger

Many studies confirm the therapeutic benefits of touch for newborns (Field, Schanberg, & Scafidi 1986; Morrow, Field, & Scafidi 1991; Scafidi, Field, & Schanberg 1990). Touch is also needed to support and sustain healthy brain development (Shore 1997). Neurochemical mechanisms seem to account at least in part for the powerful therapeutic effects of touch separate from a parent's or other caregiver's nurturing presence. Touch, particularly skin-to-skin contact, acts to stimulate or suppress the release of powerful hormones and other chemicals that affect a variety of functions in the body, including emotions, behavior, growth, and thinking.

Oxytocin is a hormone and brain neurotransmitter, whose main function is to cause the mother's uterine contractions during labor and milk flow during breastfeeding. In the birthing context, it stimulates the maternal instinct specifically; but in humans generally, oxytocin increases the trust impulse and reduces feelings of fear, fostering social bonding (Barker 2005). It helps protect the body against damage from stress by lowering blood pressure and cortisol levels, increasing tolerance to pain, and reducing anxiety; it also influences secretion of the growth hormone (Moberg 2003). Among other triggers, touch stimulates the release of oxytocin. The best chemical response comes from repetitive and soothing touch, such as massage.

Cortisol. At least through its effect on oxytocin, touch lowers levels of the stress hormone, cortisol (Blackwell 2000; Field et al. 1997a; Holden 1996; Shore 1997). Cortisol is always present in the bloodstream, but at unhealthy, high levels at times of extreme stress. In infants, high levels of cortisol damage the brain's hippocampus, which controls memory and cognition. As a result, learning is affected and mental and physical abilities decrease. Children who suffer sustained, chronically high levels of cortisol are more likely to demonstrate cognitive, social, motor, and other developmental delays (Blackwell 2000; Shore 1997). Elevated cortisol levels have been found to kill brain cells and reduce the number of cell connections, impair thinking and selective attention, and create anxious behavior (Lally & Oldershaw 2005). High levels also can contribute to physical problems later in life.

Serotonin and dopamine. Studies show that touch, in the form of massage particularly, not only decreases levels of cortisol but also increases levels of the two "feel good" brain chemicals. The first one, serotonin, helps balance mood, sleep patterns, appetite, and pain awareness (Hart 1996). Its levels in the brain can be chemically controlled with medication, but massage may help control serotonin levels naturally (Alderman 2001). The second chemical, dopamine, facilitates critical brain functions, including control of movement; memory, attention, and problem solving; and feelings of pleasure and well-being (Field et al. 2005).

Touch as tactile input to the brain

Positive human touch is not the only kind of tactile experience children need in order to develop and learn. Children also need to have touch experiences involving their physical surroundings.

The first five to seven years of life are a sensitive period for brain development. During this time, the brain is especially responsive to stimulation, which prompts a massive wiring of neurons and sculpting of brain regions. At birth, a baby's sensory regions of the brain already are well-organized and developed, with each of the senses (including touch) activating a separate part of the cerebral cortex (Prairie 2005).

Sensory input comprises the majority of an infant's learning during the first two years of life. Young children need a wide variety of ordinary experiences during their early years—including opportunities to touch objects and to move about and explore their environment. Increased motor functioning such as crawling, picking up and passing toys, and walking, for example, all support an infant's ability to seek and gain vital sensory input (Piaget 1952). As a result of millions of years of evolution, the brain of a young child *expects* to encounter these tactile experiences, and only if it does will it develop normally (Berk 2006).

Touch in social and emotional development

Just as children's physical and cognitive development requires input from tactile experiences, so too does their social and emotional development. The most influential aspect of emotional development that caring human touch especially helps forge is attachment. Attachment and touch experiences also play roles in fostering self-control, self-regulation, and other elements of social competence.

Touch for attachment

In the 1940s, John Bowlby began investigating a child's tendency to seek closeness to a primary caregiver and feel secure when that person is present—a tendency that develops when a child is given consistent, warm, and respon-

---

The Genetics of "Cute"

Human babies are born basically helpless. Because infants require so much care just to survive, natural selection has favored biological traits that evoke a caregiving response. That the oxytocin released during childbirth also triggers a maternal impulse is one example. Another is *kinderschema*, the biologically compelling nature of infantile features. Like the faces of puppies, kittens, and other animals that cannot take care of themselves from birth, a human baby's flatter face, rounder nose, bigger eyes (a baby's eyes occupy a third of its face, an adult only a fifth), and softer hair and skin compared with an adult face typically provoke a biological impulse to protect and nurture. Some experts believe that a baby's cuddly and kissable features evolved specifically as a means of obtaining needed touch from caregivers (Levy & Orlans 1998).

---

sive attention by the caregiver during the first year of life. He referred to this phenomenon as *attachment*. Many others have also studied attachment and its effects, finding that in virtually all cultures, children form strong attachments as a result of warm and responsive care (Ainsworth et al. 1978). To lack this special bond with a primary caregiver puts a child's lifelong emotional and social success at risk (Bowlby [1969] 2000).

The foundation for attachment is an established bond of trust between primary caregiver and child. That is, when the caregiver consistently is sensitive to what the infant needs (closeness, food, rest, relief, diaper change, reassurance) and responds appropriately to meet that need, the baby learns to trust that the world is a predictable and caring place. Infants communicate their needs in the only way they can—they cry. In this way, "the multiple exchanges of crying signals and caregiving responses make crying a primary vehicle for the establishment and maintenance of the attachment tie" (Ainsworth et al. 1978: 7).

Secure attachment. When a child's attachment to a parent or other primary caregiver is successful and healthy in this way, she is said to be *securely attached* to that person. Securely attached children use their primary caregiver as their point of refuge. A secure attachment allows children to venture out into the world to explore, learn, and grow, knowing someone they trust is looking after them. For infants, that trust begins with the reassurance of touch (Furman & Kennell 2000). Skin-to-skin contact, being cradled or carried, and soothing massage are all forms of the touch that infants crave. In one study (Anisfeld et al. 1990), infants carried in soft slings on their caregivers' chests were significantly more likely to be securely attached to the caregiver than infants carried in hard infant seats were. In the United States, 4-month-olds spend about 40% of their waking hours in car seats (Hewlett 2006).

Attachment, while it does start to form at birth, builds in stages throughout the baby's first year. During the first stage, most infants are friendly and welcoming to most anyone willing to meet their physical and emotional needs. Between the ages of 4 and 6 months, though, babies begin to prefer particular caregivers. It is not until around 6 months that a baby enters a third stage of attachment and shows definite preferences for a particular caregiver and expresses some distress when that caregiver is absent. This last stage of attachment is supported by a caregiver who has learned to read and understand the infant's signals, and so can sense when enough touch has been provided. At this stage, babies are easily overstimulated, so sensitive responses to them are critical (Boyd & Bee 2006).

As Alice S. Honig describes, "a well-cuddled baby with an available and intimately tuned-in caregiver is more likely to feel secure enough to toddle off on splendid adventures" (2002: 16). In their independent explorations, children develop behaviors that help lead to later social competence. Children with secure attachments are better able to balance their emotions (self-regulate) and are more likely to grow up to be confident, independent learners with strong social skills (Honig 2002).

Insecure attachment. When a child's physical and emotional needs are not met with caring and nurturing, secure attachment can fail to form; this result is termed *insecure attachment.* An infant's needs can fail to be met for a variety of reasons, including the caregiver's insensitivity or indifference or drug or alcohol abuse, physical or emotional abuse and neglect, and violence or emotional trauma within the family. Unpredictable switches between multiple caregivers can also be a factor, as can erratic caregiver behavior (Honig 1998, 2002; Levy & Orlans 1998).

Bowlby (1980) suggests that once an infant forms a secure attachment it is maintained throughout later childhood and becomes a model for new attachments. But it may be that a child's attachment security can be negatively affected after infancy by stresses such as death, divorce, and drug or alcohol abuse and a caregiver's reaction to those stresses. Children's attachment seems to be particularly vulnerable at the age of about 24 months and again at about 58 months (Bar-Haim et al. 2000). It is interesting to speculate about what is happening in children's lives at these times, and whether changes in patterns of touch are having an impact. Many American families begin toilet learning with their children around age 2, and the consistent physical contact that occurs with diapering declines. Then around age 5, children go off to primary school, where positive physical contact almost always falls off markedly, as compared with early care settings. Touch for a school-age child might decrease for a variety of reasons: parents or the child thinking he is now "too old" for cuddling and hugging, and fewer teachers per classroom, as well as the culture of the elementary school.

The ramifications of insecure attachment are deep and harmful. Children may exhibit a myriad of emotional problems, including low self-esteem, lack of self-control, and neediness and clinging (Levy & Orlans 1998). Children with insecure attachment are often characterized as angry or aggressive, engaging in acts physically harmful to themselves and to others; at times they may exhibit aggression by destroying property (Field 1999; Levy & Orlans 1998). Some researchers have noted that the most violent societies tend to be those where children grow up with less frequent positive touch and more prevalent use of punitive touch, while "high-touch" societies frequently have lower rates of violence (Field 1999; Prescott 1975). And some believe that insecure or weak attachment is the cause of the condition "failure to thrive" described earlier (Hockenberry, Wilson, & Winkelstein 2005).

Touch for developing social skills in play

When properly supervised, touch in the form of "rough-and-tumble" play can provide young children with wonderful opportunities for positive physical contact. It also is a venue for developing social skills and relationships. During rough-and-tumble play, children verbalize their feelings to their friends and participating adults, and they respond to the verbal requests of others. Children may say, for example, "You're holding me too tight!" or "No,

let me go!" Learning to both verbalize personal touch preferences and respect those communicated by others enhances a child's social relationships in early childhood and throughout life.

Often viewed by families and early childhood educators as an outlet for children's aggression, rough-and-tumble play "is largely distinct from aggression" (Smith 1995: 5). While such play-fighting may look like real fighting—in that children are wrestling, pushing, rolling, grappling, and chasing each other—"it is accompanied by laughter, smiling, and friendship" (Smith 1995: 5).

Rough-and-tumble play is a type used most widely by boys, but girls also engage in various forms of such play. It is also the common play style for male teachers interacting with young children, primarily boys, and is an important means of male socialization (Pellegrini & Smith 1998). (More on rough-and-tumble play in **Chapter Three.**)

Touch for supporting self-regulation

Touch, particularly in the form of massage, can help children self-regulate by reducing negative emotions. Studies in Sweden, for example, where massage is practiced in the schools, find that students report less aggressive and angry feelings following the massage sessions. During these sessions, the children have the option of exchanging 15-minute massages; most choose to participate. Comments reported about the massage include, "I was angry and sad and did not want to go to school. That morning we had massage. Afterward I felt sad, but not angry anymore" and "I feel more friendly after I have given the massage" (Berggren 2004: 68).

Touch supports self-regulation in other ways, too—through both its hormonal effects and the feelings of trust and security that result from reciprocal touch. That is, learning to self-regulate is hard, but it is easier when the brain is sending the child messages that say "I'm calm," and when the child knows a mistake in self-regulating will be received with understanding and positive physical affection.

Touch matters

Some teachers and caregivers may come to the subject of touch thinking, "Sure, children need some touch. But let's be reasonable. What's so *crucial* about touch for young children?" As the research described in this chapter makes clear, touch is absolutely required for proper physical and cognitive development, it offers powerful therapeutic benefits, the brain craves it, it is critical to forming secure attachments, and it fosters social and emotional development. Moreover, for each study cited or example offered here, many more could have been.

In other words, it is the purpose of this chapter to dispel all notions that teachers, caregivers, program administrators, or families may have had that touch is a *want*, not a *need*. That it is just a "feel good" kind of thing. Instead, readers should put down this chapter convinced, beyond a shadow of a doubt: *Touch is both a physiological and a psychological need. As educators we don't provide nearly enough of it, and without it horrible consequences await children.*

Nurturing Children through Touch

To decide on a preschool for her 4-year-old, Marcia is visiting several centers. In the first program she visits, the classroom is very attractive and well equipped, and the teachers are friendly and helpful in answering Marcia's questions. As she observes, Marcia notices that the teachers talk pleasantly with the children but rarely touch them. Three children listening to a story are sitting on the rug, while the teacher sits in a chair across from them. Even when a child is crying, the teacher doesn't offer physical comfort of any kind. On asking about this, Marcia is told that the center has a policy of minimal touch.

After having this experience on her first visit, Marcia is struck by a very different atmosphere in the second program she visits. Here, too, a teacher is reading to a small group of children, but they are all snuggled up with her on the couch, two on each side. Coming in a bit late, a boy happily announces, "I'm here," and then runs first to one teacher and then the other for warm hugs. When the assistant teacher intervenes in an argument between two girls, she puts an arm around the shoulder of each and helps them to calm down and talk things through.

Marcia sees positive things about both programs, but the second seems to her to be far more nurturing, and she decides to send her son there. It's a good decision. The most important single characteristic of an early childhood program is the quality of teachers' interaction with children. Children do not thrive and learn if they do not feel cared for. Describing what parents should look for in a preschool, Dodge and Bickart (1998) explain: "Young children

Fostering Attachment with Touch

Even though attachment usually refers to the bond developed between parent and child, such relationships can and *should* occur in children's out-of-home care, as well. As discussed in **Chapter Two,** forming a strong, secure attachment to their caregiver makes children feel competent and capable to explore and develop emotionally. Attachments formed between children and out-of-home caregivers also can compensate for weaker bonds between a child and the caregiver at home (Honig 2002; Mitchell-Copeland, Denham, & DeMulder 1997; Waters & Cummings 2000).

Infants, toddlers, and preschoolers all are capable of forming secure attachments to their caregivers in early education settings (Baker & Manfredi/Petitt 2004; Honig 2002; Mitchell-Copeland, Denham, & DeMulder 1997; Waters & Cummings 2000). But this does not mean that they always *will.* They are most likely to bond if cared for in a high-quality setting.

High-quality care shares certain characteristics. For one, changes of caregivers should be predictable and infrequent, and each teacher should care for only a limited number of children (Baker & Manfredi/Petitt 2004; NAEYC 2005b). NAEYC's *Accreditation Criteria,* for example, specifies teacher-child ratios for various group sizes (see www.naeyc.org/accreditation/criteria/teacher_child_ratios.html). High-quality care is also characterized by children having access to developmentally appropriate toys, materials, experiences, and relationships, especially teacher-child relationships that are warm, responsive, and individualized (Copple & Bredekamp 2006; NAEYC 1997, 2005a, 2005b). Positive, nurturing touch is key to promoting such relationships.

live in the moment; when they have hurt feelings or bodies, they need a responsive adult right away. As a parent, you would not dream of ignoring your crying child; you want a teacher who will offer the same degree of comfort and security. Children need to know that school is a safe, caring place" (12).

For most of us, whatever our age, when we are given a gentle touch on the shoulder or a friendly hug, we feel good about who we are and know we are cared for. Young children spend many hours in group settings, and they cannot wait until they get home at night to get the message that they are cared for and valued. Touch is not the only thing that communicates this message, but it is a very important one. To give children warm touches, hold them on your lap, and respond caringly when they are in distress is to give them the essential ingredients to a healthy sense of self—making them feel valued, nurtured, and safe.

Creating this kind of classroom atmosphere and interaction is so vital to high-quality care that the National Association for the Education of Young Children (NAEYC) has made such interaction a requirement for an early childhood program to be accredited. The association's *Early Childhood Program Standards and Accreditation Criteria* (2005b) offers the following measure of quality care:

> 1.B.02—Teaching staff express warmth through behaviors such as physical affection, eye contact, tone of voice, and smiles. . . . 1.B.05—Teaching staff function as secure bases for children. They respond promptly in developmentally appropriate ways to children's positive initiations, negative emotions, and feelings of hurt and fear by providing comfort, support, and assistance. . . . 1.B.07—Teaching staff evaluate and change their responses based on individual needs. Teaching staff vary their interactions to be sensitive and responsive to differing abilities, temperaments, activity levels, and cognitive and social development.

Similarly, evaluators for the Child Development Associate (CDA) credential look for evidence that:

> Candidate uses positive messages, such as holding out hand, hugging, smiling, to communicate frequently with child. Candidate gives and accepts lots of hugs, kisses, and snuggles to give children the message that each person is important, respected, and valued. Candidate shows acceptance, respect, and sensitivity to each child's feelings to help children develop a sense of security. (Council for Professional Recognition 1999)

These guidelines are not unique to the United States. For example, families, teachers, and service providers in New Zealand are guided to look for the following as indicators of remarkable quality in early care and education:

> The adults regard physical contact and closeness with children as natural and essential. They show they are at ease with a child who wants to sit on their knee, hold their hand, or have a cuddle. In play, you may see children getting piggy-backs or being lifted up to reach a ball from a tree. You may see an adult with his/her arm around a child while reading a book. You will see children sometimes get a congratulatory hug when they have a personal achievement. Non-mobile babies especially are carried around and given lots of physical interaction and touch when they are not having floor play/exercise time. (Farquhar 2005: 45)

To conduct themselves in ways that are both respectful and nurturing, teachers clearly need to be aware of what types of touches the various children in their classroom appreciate and which they do not. These likes and dislikes will depend on the particular child, her cultural and family experiences, and her relationship with that teacher.

Developmentally appropriate touch

As in any area of practice, effective practitioners making decisions about incorporating touch in their program must reflect on what is age appropriate, individually appropriate, and culturally appropriate (Bredekamp & Copple 1997; Copple & Bredekamp 2006; NAEYC 1997). For example, lap-sitting and rocking may be age appropriate for a toddler, but may not be for a school-age child. A backrub may be appropriate for some preschoolers, but not for all. A hug between a female teacher and a male child may be culturally appropriate

---

Patterns of Touch—By Age

Research conducted in infant/toddler and preschool settings shows that infants daily receive more positive touch from their caregivers than toddlers and preschoolers do. This difference probably results from infants needing a lot more hands-on routine care, such as cleaning, diapering, and feeding, and because nonmobile infants must be carried so much of the time. In contrast, preschoolers receive more negative touch than infants or toddlers do from their caregivers, typically to redirect or control their behavior (Cigales et al. 1996).

Infants and toddlers receive little if any positive touch from their peers (Cigales et al. 1996). Nonmobile infants rarely have physical contact with other infants, and toddlers tend to play side by side instead of collaboratively with other toddlers. Also, toddlers are at a stage when they are experimenting with different types of touches. Until they learn which touches are pleasurable to themselves and others, their experiments can make for some pretty negative physical contact (pushing, pulling, pinching, biting, grabbing, squeezing) for other children within their reach.

Preschoolers, however, do touch each other positively (Field et al. 1994). And by age 3 or 4, children are better able to discriminate in touching or avoiding body parts that other children find "vulnerable," or don't like touched (Cigales et al. 1996; Jones & Yarbrough 1985). (See **Chapter Four** for discussion of vulnerable parts of the body.) The hesitation to touch vulnerable parts is thought to mimic adult behavior, reflecting what preschoolers have learned from their adult caregivers about how, where, and when to touch (Jones & Yarbrough 1985).

---

in the United States generally, but not for children who follow a faith that considers touch appropriate only between members of the same sex.

These examples are all occasions of touch between teacher and child. Touch between children in a classroom and touch in the form of tactile experiences with objects in the environment also call for these considerations of what is developmentally appropriate.

Considering age and individual differences

Throughout this chapter and the next, considerations and guidelines for touch that is age appropriate are described separately for infants, toddlers, preschoolers, and kindergartners, whenever that discrimination is useful.

Helping to meet a child's individual physical, emotional, and cultural needs is key to implementing developmentally appropriate practice. When we consider what touches may or may not be appropriate for young children, we should draw on an "ethic of care"—that is, a mindset that embraces personal, relationship-specific responsibilities and ways of caring for each other (Noddings [1984] 2003). Interactions with children must be based on individual relationships, reflecting a particular child's specific wishes and needs. When we are responsive to each child individually, we help children to develop a positive sense of body awareness and empower them with a strong sense of body ownership (more on these two concepts in **Chapter Four**). (These individual differences are at their most extreme in children with touch-related special needs, as described in **Chapter Six**.)

Considering culture

Finally, teachers also must keep in mind that the social and cultural contexts in which children live affect the kinds of physical interaction that children and their families find acceptable. For example, many teachers routinely touch children on the top or back of the head. However, in some

Patterns of Touch—By Gender

A child's gender can influence how that child is touched and how often. Preschool boys are touched more often by adults than are preschool girls (Cigales et al. 1996), and the majority of all adult touch that boys receive comes from women (Field et al. 1994; Harrison-Speake & Willis 1995; Major, Schmidlin, & Williams 1990; Perdue & Connor 1978). Why do boys receive more touch than girls? It could be that their predominantly female caregivers perceive boys as having a greater need for redirection or restraining, and that boys engage more often than girls in tickling, friendly rough-housing, and active play with male caregivers.

In both boys and girls, desire for closeness and cuddling with adult caregivers decreases with age and results in less physical contact with caregivers overall (Harrison-Speake & Willis 1995; Weisberg 1975). By preschool age, for both boys and girls, the majority of positive touch given and received is between children, rather than between children and a caregiver (Field et al. 1994). Another difference in touch by gender is that girls' aggression is primarily verbal, while boys' aggression is primarily physical (Gartrell 2004).

Male staff members are particularly affected by issues of gender in early childhood environments, due to society's disproportionate fear of their touching children inappropriately. In some programs, male educators might be forbidden any physical contact with children, especially those under the age of 2. They might not be allowed to diaper a child, for example. This is particularly unfortunate because there is "a high correlation between child and male positive touch, indicating that more positive touch between children involves males" (Field et al. 1994: 118). This male toddler teacher is a good example:

> I'm very lucky, in that I have no special restrictions on what I can do at work because of my sex. I change diapers, pick up children, hold them on my lap while reading or to comfort them, and tickle them while we're playing. I know that touch is a very important communication tool for all of us, but especially for babies and toddlers. Sometimes it's the only way they can let you know how they feel or learn how you respond to them.

Chapter Five discusses the fear many teachers and other staff have of allegations of abuse, which discourages many men from entering the education field altogether (Nelson 2002; Rice & Goessling 2005). It also describes how programs—by proactively setting touch policies—can allow and encourage touch *and at the same time* protect children and staff. Proactive policies, actions, and guidance especially help male teachers feel more comfortable touching children (Nelson 2004).

Asian cultures Buddhist beliefs say the head is sacred and touching it is taboo. Conversely, failing to touch the head of a child from a Mexican background could be deemed an insult (Small 1998). This cultural variation in touching is an important consideration if patting a child's head is part of a teacher's regular routine. For a teacher to give a hug or backrub to a child from certain cultural backgrounds could cause great discomfort. Instead of either avoiding physical contact entirely or using it indiscriminately, teachers must determine on an individual basis whether or not a touch will be considered appropriate and then interact accordingly.

Not only are there cross-cultural considerations in the use of touch; there are variations within any given culture, as well. Teachers should avoid applying cultural generalizations without getting to know children and their families individually. Afford privacy, respect for the body, and autonomy in relation to a child's cultural background and expectations (Ahn & Gilbert 1992). A program should involve the child's family by informing family members that touch is a valued part of its practice and by asking about their cultural and

A Touch Test for Teachers

The Touch Test is a tool teachers can use to help themselves become more sensitive to what constitutes appropriate touch (Del Prete 1998). When a child is new to a program, that child and that teacher are strangers. Instead of assuming the appropriate level of touch and physical affection generally, the teacher should take time to find out what the child wants and expects, just like she would with anyone she were meeting and getting to know for the first time. In other words, the Touch Test helps her set a baseline for touch with a new child.

The Touch Test is simple. As she considers what touch to use with an unfamiliar child, the teacher simply asks herself: "Would this touch be appropriate if I gave it to a stranger?" For example, a handshake would be appropriate with a stranger, while a prolonged hug would not be.

familial practices and preferences. This can be done initially through pre-enrollment procedures, such as questionnaires. Learning about family expectations and practices during enrollment and afterward will help teachers respond accordingly from the beginning of their relationship with the child. (For sample letters and a family questionnaire, see **Appendix C.**)

Teachers may wonder what to do when children's comfort or discomfort with a certain form of physical interaction is at odds with what they will experience in mainstream American society. For example, let's say a child is from a culture that emphasizes formality between children and adults outside the family. Having learned this information from the family, the teacher might begin with the assumption that she should not hug this child. But she could find that the child, seeing other children getting warm hugs, wants to be hugged too and has his feelings hurt if he is not. This situation is one to discuss with the family. Once they understand how the child is reacting, his parents may be comfortable having the child get hugs at school even though this practice wouldn't be acceptable to them within their own cultural circle.

Just as children can learn that the food they eat or the language they speak at home differs from that at school, they can learn that different patterns of physical interaction are acceptable in different contexts. In other instances, families may stand firm in objecting to some kinds of physical touch being given to their child at school. Teachers can discuss with the family what they can do instead to make sure the child feels cared for.

Being reflective about touch

Clearly there are issues of some complexity that arise as the early childhood field thinks about the important goals of creating a nurturing environment and at the same time ensuring that there are no touch-related threats to the welfare of children or staff. Because of the importance and complexity of such issues, every practitioner needs to engage in thoughtful reflection about them. Critical, too, is discussion among a program's staff and leadership, and, at times, with early childhood professionals in other programs and with the families being served. Some of the questions that are fruitful for consideration are listed in the box **Questions to Talk Over in Your Program** opposite.

Touch throughout the day

> There is a child in my classroom who needs me to be close to him when he's working, or he has a hard time getting his work done. But he doesn't like me to be too close. If he's sitting at the computer, he wants me to sit with our shoulders touching, and that's close enough.
>
> One day, we were sitting side-by-side at the computer station. He needed my assistance with the keyboard, so I stretched my left arm around his back in order to reach the keyboard, placing my left hand on top of his left hand. After showing him what to do, I pulled my arm back around to my side. He reached down, picked up my hand, and drew my arm back around his waist. I left my arm around him for the rest of the time we worked at the computer.
>
> —An assistant teacher

Positive touch easily can—and *should*—be included in the daily routines and activities of all early childhood programs. Some of the following ways, such as incorporating touch in music and movement activities, are probably already common in most classrooms. Others may not be as common.

Many factors affect whether various uses of touch are appropriate and effective in an early childhood education setting. What is the learning goal, and how might adding or increasing the quality or quantity of touch serve that goal? Do caregivers and teachers know the children's touch preferences? A responsive caregiver will use this information and react to what individual children find comfortable and nonintrusive. Adults must be mindful of both verbal and nonverbal cues from children and let these signals guide physical

Questions to Talk Over in Your Program

What kinds of touch do the children experience in our program day in and day out, from adults and from one another? In thinking about this question, and perhaps doing some observation, we will want to consider all forms of touch, including situations in which children are touched for a utilitarian function, such as diapering, or to manage their behavior, such as physically separating children who are fighting.

What kind of "touch environment" do we want to have? In other words, what kinds of touch are we sure that we want to see in this program? What kinds of touch are we sure we would *not* want to occur? Are there gray areas we should discuss? What factors should we consider in making these judgments and carrying them out from day to day?

In our program are we avoiding or minimizing touch? If so, why is this? Do we consciously or unconsciously limit touch from male caregivers?

Are we clear in our policies and guiding principles about touch? Have any problems or complaints arisen in the past that are not addressed in our policies or that could be better addressed? [If there isn't a no-touch policy]

Do both children and staff feel that our environment is welcoming, encouraging, and safe? What guidelines and safeguards should we have in place to ensure that touch is appropriate and both children and staff feel safe?

What can we do to incorporate more positive, nurturing touch into our day? How can we incorporate touch into routines where touch is now absent and make it a natural part of our day?

Are we encouraging body awareness and healthy sexuality development? Are we teaching children about inappropriate versus appropriate touch and that they have control over the touch they receive? If not, how can we accomplish this?

What are our goals for the children from cultural backgrounds in which feelings or beliefs about touch or personal space differ significantly from the norms in American culture? How can we involve the families in this discussion?

What is my own level of comfort with touch? How much personal space do I need to feel comfortable? How am I communicating my personal touch preferences to the children in my care?

interactions. Children will let us know which tactile experiences they find comfortable, as well as when, where, and how they want to be touched.

As important as touch is in the classroom, sometimes a teacher can go overboard. For example, "a child who is absorbed in building a block tower may not appreciate the praise and pats of a hovering teacher if they interrupt [the child's] concentration" (Twardosz & Nordquist 1983: 149). When children are actively engaged, the teacher should keep her focus on maintaining that engagement.

In arranging opportunities for children to experience touch through their play, for example, she should provide materials that support touch, such as fabric, cardboard boxes, carpet squares, pieces of foam, blocks, and the like. Then, as the children play, the teacher can call their attention to the tactile sensations they are experiencing and help them articulate what they are feeling without interrupting the activity. Being mindful of children's activity levels, as well as the intended purposes of the physical contact, is key to incorporating touch successfully.

Interpersonal touch and other tactile experiences have a role to play in everything that happens in an early childhood program. The following sections look at some important or particularly pertinent classroom routines and activities through that lens. Most of the suggestions are appropriate for preschool and older children. But infants and toddlers are included in the discussion of greetings and rest time. Activities and materials for infants and toddlers also are covered in **Chapter Four.**

The next chapter is also where the idea of respecting children's inherent right to control when, where, and how they are touched is developed and detailed guidance for teachers is offered. In general, a teacher should know the child will welcome a touch before giving it. Asking and getting the child's permission before touching is one way to ensure the touch will be accepted. This is especially useful when the child and teacher don't yet know and trust each other, and less necessary once a teacher and child have developed a trusting relationship and know each other's touch preferences. For most children, for example, touches on some body parts feel more or less uncomfortable than on others.

Greetings

A teacher's first opportunity of the day for adding touch to her practice is during the morning greeting time. For infants and some toddlers, the parent would probably hand the child into the arms of the teacher, after a good-bye kiss; and the teacher might talk with him and walk him around the room a bit to ease the transition. For older children, as parent and child enter the classroom, the teacher can touch the child in greeting and to communicate her happiness that the child has arrived. Many teachers already do this, but it helps to think about it consciously. A teacher might think she greets children this way more often than she actually does, or she may find that she is inconsistent from child to child or day to day.

A good place to touch most children in greeting is their shoulder or back, which generally are two areas that feel least vulnerable to most children (Jones & Yarbrough 1985; Neill 1991). Touching the child can also serve as an informal health check for conditions such as a temperature, swollen glands, or profuse sweating (Aronson 2002). But some children may not like their head or neck being touched.

Group gatherings

Morning meeting or circle time can incorporate touch concepts in comfortable, nonintrusive ways. As children gather, the teacher should pay attention to nonverbal cues that they may be crowding too close for comfort, and use it as an opportunity for practice at boundary setting. She might encourage them to express their comfort or discomfort by saying things such as, "You're sitting too close. Please move over" or "You can sit next to me; I have room."

She also might use the **Personal Bubble** exercise (see box below) to explore and foster discussion of the concept of personal space.

Children shouldn't be forced to sit too close for their individual comfort. The teacher can observe children's comfort levels and plan circle logistics accordingly. This might mean gathering smaller groups of children together or placing children in a larger area. She might want to consider providing each child with an individual carpet square to place and sit on, with the understanding that each can put his square as close to or as far away from other children's squares as he wishes, provided it doesn't make anyone else uncomfortable.

Storytime provides both formal (e.g., in planned group time) and informal (e.g., when a child climbs up with a book to sit next to the teacher during free time) opportunities for touch by both teachers and children. Instead of

---

Personal Bubble Exercise

The Personal Bubble exercise (Adams & Fay 1981; Hart-Rossi 1984) is useful for helping children (older preschoolers and up) become more aware of personal space and comfort zones. (This same exercise can be used with teachers and family members, as is the case in the training session **Teaching Children about Appropriate Touch** outlined in **Appendix D.**)

To begin, group the children in pairs. Have them stand across the room from each other; for younger children, about four feet away is enough. One child in the pair stands still, while the other begins stepping toward the standing partner. As soon as the standing child begins to feel uncomfortable, he says, Stop! Both partners then discuss why the standing child felt the moving partner came too close. To prompt that discussion, ask questions such as: "How did you feel when you knew she was too close?" "How did your body feel when you thought he was too close to you?" "What were you thinking when she got closer?"

Do this activity one pair at a time so each child can focus on the feeling of the partner being too close. When multiple pairs do this activity simultaneously, the children are distracted by what they see the other children doing and they stop focusing on their own feelings.

---

large groups that require a lot of sitting still and listening, a teacher might consider informal storytimes of two or three children each that focus on sharing and enjoying a story together. She could let the children sit on her lap or curl up to her side, as long as it is comfortable for everyone. This adult-child interaction also lends itself to greater warmth and responsiveness, which also promote literacy development. Reading aloud to young children remains one of the most important activities for building literacy (Neuman, Copple, & Bredekamp 2000; Trelease 2001; Willmarth 2001).

Activities

Music and movement activities offer many opportunities for positive touch. Classic games such as Head, Shoulders, Knees, and Toes promote body awareness; and songs and games in which children swing arms, hold hands, and clap each other's hands provide positive and appropriate physical contact (Pirtle 1998). When an activity calls for holding hands, children should be allowed to regulate the physical contact by choosing whether to hold hands or maybe wrists or fingers instead. A noncompetitive game of Musical Chairs (where a chair is removed each time the music stops, but no child is eliminated) is another fun physical activity—most children enjoy the gentle rough-and-tumble play of trying to all sit together in a smaller and smaller space.

Art activities provide great opportunities for exploring physical sensation, especially tactile exploration. Children naturally love to explore art media such as finger paints, playdough, sand, glue, water, and collage materials. They can explore the different sensations on their own, or they can collaborate with others—for example, by spreading paint, clay, or sand on each other's hands or arms to see what that feels like (Bos 1978). Both children must be willing participants, of course. Children can also try painting with different body parts—each hand, their feet, elbows, head. Teachers will want to be flexible when encouraging children to paint with their feet, however; feet are often vulnerable body parts, and the paint could feel uncomfortable to some.

Handling objects of different textures offers rich experiences with touch. Objects covered or made out of velvet, chenille, felt, silk, leather, synthetic fur, cotton, and wool all provide unique tactile stimulation, as does play with water, sand, cornmeal, birdseed, cornstarch, flour, foam, and other materials. Teachers can encourage children to stroke each other's arms with the objects and then discuss how it feels.

Pet center

Keeping a classroom pet, such as a rabbit or a guinea pig, can also encourage positive touch. Certainly, such an addition should be undertaken with caution, as some children might be allergic to animal dander; but a pet in the classroom has many benefits. The simple act of stroking an animal's fur can provide soothing tactile stimulation. When children interact with pets, stress indicators such as heart rate, blood pressure, and cortisol levels all decrease (Kaminski, Pellino, & Wish 2002).

Classroom rules about caring for the pet should include that the children must respect the animal's right not to be touched inappropriately—roughly, carelessly, or anytime the animal shows it doesn't want to be touched. Children gain respect for the personal boundaries of others when they experience these with pets and practice responding sensitively to the animal's preferences.

Physical play

Movement games, such as parachute games, dancing, and ball toss games, can encourage positive touch. Good too are "three-legged" games in which two children must maneuver together as one body. When playing Simon Says, the teacher can request movements such as "Simon says shake your friend's hand" or "Simon says pat your friend gently on the back." Children can hold hands or link arms for relay races. Teachers may need to give guidance about touch during more rowdy play so the play remains appropriate. They might need, for example, to have rules during Tag such as "Only touches on the shoulder" or "Touch with the tips of your fingers and not with the palm of your hand."

A form of physical play that needs special discussion is rough-and-tumble play, or play-fighting. As discussed in **Chapter Two,** touch in the form of rough-and-tumble play offers multiple benefits, including as a vehicle for practicing social interaction and as a wonderful opportunity for appropriate touch. Rough-and-tumble play is used most widely by boys, but girls also engage in various forms of it. It is also a common play style for male teachers interacting with young children, primarily boys, and is believed to play an important role in male socialization (Pellegrini & Smith 1998).

During rough-and-tumble play, physical contact occurs in a nonaggressive fashion and typically includes pushing from the front, pushing from the back, holding and grabbing, wrestling and pinning, chasing and running, and falling down (Scott & Panksepp 2003).

Rough-and-tumble play is naturally very physical. Teachers have to be selective about where and when they let it happen (maybe not inside the classroom, or only on floor mats; outdoors only where the ground is soft) and monitor it. Yet much of this physical contact is appropriate touch—that is, its purpose is clear, children choose to be touched, the tone is positive. Also, it usually involves nonvulnerable body parts such as arms, shoulders, and backs, and thus raises few problems for children, as long as no one is likely to get hurt. Because rough-and-tumble play is usually initiated, orchestrated, and completed by the children themselves, they usually find it enjoyable rather than threatening. Children can engage in this boisterous activity with varying amounts of physical contact; for example, running and chasing are considered rough-and-tumble play, but relatively little touching is involved. That children have control over such a physically active type of play reinforces to them that they can and should have power over how and when their bodies are touched.

Rough-and-tumble play is by definition nonaggressive. For example, play-hitting is done lightly and with a flat, open palm (like in Tag), while aggressive hitting would use a closed fist and greater power. Although rough-and-tumble play between children often appears forceful, observing teachers usually can just monitor the play without having to interfere. However, such play-fighting can sometimes cross the invisible line to actual fighting, where both bodies and feelings can be hurt. Teachers should always intervene if children begin hitting with closed fists or trying to inflict physical pain, or if other children in the environment feel threatened or are in danger of being hurt by accident. If teachers are themselves participants in the play, they should stop it immediately if it gets too rough or its tone turns negative.

Rough-and-tumble play is an opportunity to practice boundary setting, too. Children should be taught to say, "I've had enough" or "That's too rough!" to either their peers or the adults. The teacher's role is to act as a protective presence, helping children involve their bodies in positive physical contact while setting their own limits.

Rest time

Leading up to and at the beginning of rest time are perhaps the most natural and obvious times to incorporate more positive touch into the daily routine. There may be a few infants who need to be mellowed and soothed before being placed in their cribs to sleep. Walking a baby around, rocking her for a time, or rubbing her back can help her relax and get ready to sleep.

Older children can be helped to relax on their cots or mats by being stroked, patted, or massaged on their backs, shoulders, or other areas individual children find soothing, such as the face. Only nonvulnerable body parts are touched, and the child can accept or decline the teacher's offer—in words, if the child is older, or with verbal or physical cues, for infants or toddlers. Older children can also be taught these same methods, which they then may want to use to help themselves or another child relax. If both children are agreeable, this peer interaction is something teachers will generally want to allow. Clearly, touch should cease if a child expresses discomfort.

Massage

Massage has been shown to offer therapeutic benefits from the birth onward. It is often used as a therapy to help relieve certain problems, and it can be routinely used in early childhood programs for general relaxation and stress relief. (For more on the therapeutic effects of massage, see **Chapter Two**. Also see the **Resources** section for books and Web sites about infant massage.) A program that uses massage should state this fact in its family handbook and discuss during orientation how and why it uses massage with children. The program might offer families training, too, so they can use massage at home.

For the massage to be appropriate, permission must be requested of and granted by the child each time. The touch should be firm, not ticklish or hard. As the teacher models respect and appropriate touch to the child, the child learns to give respectful and appropriate touch to others.

Infants enjoy massage when they are in a quiet alert state. With infants, the teacher asks permission by looking the baby in the eyes, showing her hands, and asking, "Would you like a massage?" Smiles, wiggles, and waving arms would signal the child's desire for and acceptance of the touch. The teacher's hands should be room temperature; too cold or hot can scare an infant. When the baby shows signs of no longer wanting massage, such as frowning, squirming, or crying, the teacher should honor those cues. A teacher should massage only the infant's back through clothing, arms, or legs. One exception might be during diapering, when a few tummy strokes can help promote regular bowel movements. A massage at home by a parent can be more intimate and involve more vulnerable body parts such as the chest, neck, or lower back.

Older children are capable of asking for or declining massage, which the teacher should encourage them to do. The teacher can do the massaging, or children can massage each other (as always, with each other's permission). Stroking an older child on the back or shoulders through his clothing is very comforting. Sometimes hugs or just a resting hand can be as comforting as stroking.

Teaching Children about Touch

The task of young children in their earliest years is to learn about themselves and the world around them. Direct experience through the senses is their means of learning, with the sense of touch one of the most significant and highly developed. As discussed in **Chapter Two,** the thoughts, feelings, and tactile sensations associated with touching and being touched give children what they need to develop and grow physically, cognitively, socially, and emotionally. A role of caregivers and teachers during this early period is to supply young children with touch experiences, as well as help them make sense of those experiences and the role of touch in society—in other words, to teach a curriculum of touch.

Body awareness

At its most basic, *body awareness* is the fundamental understanding that we have a physical self—this thing called a "body." From the moment of birth, a baby begins learning that her body is something separate from her mother's; that it has the capacity to feel sensations both internal and from the world around her; that she can use her body to move around in and act on that external world. And she begins experimenting and practicing.

The child also becomes aware that, through some combination of biology and experiences with touch, she feels discomfort (or feels "vulnerable") when certain parts of her body are touched. Generally speaking, vulnerable body parts tend to be a child's neck, chest, lower back, buttocks, genitals, legs, and feet; the most nonvulnerable parts tend to be the shoulders, back, arms, and hands (Jones & Yarbrough 1985; Neill 1991). Some body parts, such as the genitals and buttocks, tend to be the most vulnerable of these. There is, of course, variability among children; for example, it may bother some children to have their head or hair touched, but not others. Which parts typically feel vulnerable also varies somewhat among cultures and between children and adults; the face, for example, is often not as vulnerable for children as for adults (Jones & Yarbrough 1985). But which touches children prefer and allow varies from child to child, depending on their biology, past experiences, and cultural expectations. When interacting with children, caregivers should avoid touching vulnerable areas, unless it is really necessary, such as when diapering or administering first aid.

Body awareness also is a term to describe the internal body "map" each of us develops that lets us know by feel where our body is in space, what positions the various parts of our body are in, and how we are moving at any given moment. We use this body map to move in the world without having to rely on sight to guide each movement. So, for example, our body map tells us that we are stepping up onto the curb, without having to look to adjust or check our leg and foot positions. A body map develops throughout early childhood, from the millions of sensory inputs the child's brain receives from his motions. (If a child's sensory system misperceives the world or processes those perceptions inaccurately, his body cannot create an accurate body map. Such a child typically must rely heavily on his visual systems and will have problems with motor skills and in other areas. For more on what can go wrong in the body's touch system, see **Chapter Six.**)

Teachers can help young children develop their sense of body awareness in a couple of important ways. They can supply children with experiences of physical sensation of various kinds. They can talk and act with children in ways that draw children's attention to how their bodies are moving, to the physical sensations they are feeling, and to the physical control they are gaining over their bodies as they interact with the world. (Teachers also can talk and act in ways that reinforce and show respect for another kind of control: the idea that each person has an inherent right to choose when, where, and how they are touched, as discussed below in **Body Ownership.**) And teachers can prompt and encourage the children themselves to talk and act in ways that evidence their developing body awareness.

Body awareness for infants

Massage can supply a variety of physical sensations. Time can be specifically devoted to massage sessions with babies, but diapering and cleaning routines also are good times. Babies will show whether the pressure of the touch is too light, too strong, or just right. Most babies prefer a deeper pressure to a lighter pressure, which can feel unpleasant (Field, Schanberg, & Scafidi 1986). (For more about massage, see the box in **Chapter Three.**)

A caregiver can broaden the child's tactile experiences by using textured materials to touch the baby. She might stroke the baby with a piece of silk or burlap or use a handheld paper fan to gently waft air around the baby's body.

Tickling

No conversation about touch and young children would be complete without examining the role of the tickle, which has intrigued great minds for more than two thousand years. The ancient Greek philosopher Socrates wondered whether the sensation caused by tickling was pleasurable or painful, and that question basically remains unanswered still, as this early childhood education student recalls:

> As a child, tummy tickling was something I enjoyed having in small amounts when my dad tickled me and my siblings. After a few moments, though, I would ask my dad to stop because the tickling would cause me to have to go to the bathroom.

What has been determined is that there are two types of tickles: a light sensation akin to that of a bug crawling on the skin, and another caused by a deeper pressure applied repeatedly to one specific body area (such as the belly or armpits). The first kind is rarely pleasant and feels more annoying, like an itch. The second kind is the type that often causes laughter, but can be unpleasant too (Harris 1999).

As with other types of physical contact, adults must consider whether the individual child likes and wants to be tickled. Infants typically find tickling more pleasurable than older children do; however, this does not mean all infants enjoy being tickled. If the infant shows signs of discomfort, such as grimacing or squirming to get away, the tickling should stop. The same holds true for an older child: Any expression of discomfort should be taken as a sign to stop the tickle. Awareness of comfort and discomfort is a crucial part of respect for another's body.

She might also gently roll the baby, wiggle his fingers and toes, and give little pinches and pats, which all send different sensory messages. The caregiver can also begin naming each of the baby's body parts as she touches them.

Large motor activities also reinforce body awareness and help build the infant's body map. Walking, rocking, swinging, and swaying with a baby, perhaps to music, all send balance and position messages to the baby's developing brain. Bouncing gently is also a good form of stimulation: A caregiver might sit, balancing the baby on her foot, and gently bounce her leg up and down. Or she can sit on the floor, legs stretched out, balancing the baby on her knees; then, holding the baby under the arms, bounce her knees up and down. As much as possible, equipment that limits babies' ability to use their large muscles to move and balance, such as swings, high chairs, walkers, and mounted exercise chairs, should be avoided. Babies should lay, roll, crawl, and sit on the floor, where they can move freely and discover their bodies' capabilities and limitations.

Because infants can't yet say what does or doesn't feel good, a caregiver must pay attention to their sounds and nonverbal cues. She should watch for signs of pleasure or discomfort, then take that opportunity to put into words what the infant seems to be feeling. Although an infant is too young to understand much more than the tone of a caregiver's voice at that age, her responsiveness to the infant matters. It shows the baby that uncomfortable touch is not something he is supposed to learn to just tolerate. Over time, it introduces vocabulary for expressing comfort and discomfort. For example, if a baby squirms to be released from constraining clothing or coverings, the caregiver should respond by loosening them while talking about his level of comfort or discomfort: "Tight? That's wrapped too tight for you? Let me make that feel better." During diaper changes, she should verbalize for the baby what is happening to his body, and validate his expressions of comfort or discomfort by verbally acknowledging the feelings: "That wet cloth is making you feel uncomfortable" or "Now you're nice and dry."

Naming All Parts of the Body

Naming the parts of the body is a great game to play with children of all ages, although their understanding and level of participation in the game will vary with their developmental stage. It also helps promote body awareness. Young children instinctively explore all parts of their bodies, from the tops of their heads to the tips of their toes—and that includes their genitals. Such exploration is normal and part of healthy sexuality development.

Families and teachers should respond to this harmless exploration by naming the child's sexual body parts with their proper names. Using the proper names (i.e., *penis*, *vagina*, and the rest) shows respect for *all* parts of the child's body and reinforces that they are nothing to be embarrassed or secretive about, though they are private. It is also important that children know what to call their body parts, especially if they ever need to describe an inappropriate touch.

When a baby (or older children, too) conveys discomfort during diapering, dressing, and so on, the caregiver should not scold him or show annoyance. The child's right not to have to tolerate uncomfortable sensations should be respected right from the start.

Body awareness for toddlers

During the toddler years, caregivers can continue to engage children in motor and tactile activities that reinforce body awareness and help build the body map. They can create touch or sensory boards, for example, from sturdy pieces of smooth wood or foam board affixed with scraps of materials of different textures for children to touch. At times, toddlers can take off their shoes to feel different textures with their feet rather than always with their hands. Outdoors they might walk on fresh-cut grass, sand, or concrete. They might even put their feet into pans of water.

Their nonverbal cues will communicate what they feel. The role of the caregiver is to observe as the toddlers experience these sensations, then introduce them to vocabulary for such feelings: Was it *cold, gooey, rough, smooth, silky, hot, tickly, gritty, sticky, heavy, light*? Toddlers typically will still be too young to use many of these words, except maybe simpler ones such as *hot-cold, dry-wet, rough-smooth*, but the caregiver's verbalizing lays a foundation for later development. With each sensation, the caregiver also watches for nonverbal cues of the children's pleasure and displeasure with the sensation, then provides the language needed to express those feeling with words too, building on the type of language used with infants.

When a toddler is undressing, for example, the caregiver might talk about how the air feels on the child's skin or how body movements change with and without clothes, then help the child to express her feelings about those sensations with language. She can verbalize for the toddler, "It looks like that snap on your pants rubs your tummy" or "Does a backrub at naptime feel good?" It is important that children learn to attend to and understand the messages their bodies send them.

Teachers also support body awareness when they encourage toddlers to help with personal hygiene and during diapering or toileting (Ahn & Gilbert 1992; Greenman & Stonehouse 1996). For example, if a child's face needs cleaning, the teacher might try giving the child a disposable washcloth, with instructions to go to a mirror and clean herself. A toddler also can assist by removing clothing or undoing diaper tapes during diapering, or helping to wipe with a disposable cloth and washing her hands during toileting. As the child takes on some of these personal care duties, the need for the teacher to touch the child's most vulnerable body areas diminishes. As children's learning and development progress, the teacher can help them become responsible for recognizing the physical signals their bodies give them that they need to use the bathroom. Of course, toddlers will still need adults to monitor and sometimes assist with cleaning afterwards.

Body awareness for preschoolers

To help preschoolers, teachers can provide a variety of objects for children to rub and roll over their bodies, and talk with them about the way each item feels. A texture obstacle course can be designed that could have children touching, walking barefoot, or crawling over tactile materials such as lengths of sandpaper, bubble wrap, aluminum foil, cotton batting, or heavy textured vinyl. They can dig in the dirt, knead bread dough, crumple aluminum foil, stroke velvet. As they experience the varying textures, they can be encouraged to describe how each feels and to notice which sensations they prefer and why.

Preschoolers are at a prime time for learning new vocabulary and concepts. Now adults can talk with them, not to them. As the teacher watches children at play with textures and listens to the words they use, he can look for opportunities to extend their language. For example, if a child describes a blanket as *rough* and the teacher feels it and experiences *scratchy*, he could introduce this new vocabulary word. If the child says, "I don't like that" while pulling on the elastic cuff of a blouse or shirt, the teacher could probe her dislike and provide words to better describe the dislike and discomfort: "You don't like the way the elastic feels on your arm? Is it too tight? Or don't you like to feel the elastic on your skin?"

Teachers also can encourage physical play, such as children linking elbows and walking or skipping in a circle. (Rough-and-tumble play is discussed in **Chapter Three.**) Art activities are always great opportunities for tactile experiences. When using markers or painting with brushes, preschoolers could try holding the implements with body parts other than their dominant hand, such as the left hand if they are right-handed, or in the crook of their arm at the elbow. A brush can even be attached to a hat so children can paint with their heads. When children experience these different sensations, their overall body awareness is heightened.

Healthy sexuality development

Children's sexuality development is a normal part of their growing body awareness. Even before they are born, children experiment with their bodies, including their sex organs. Sexuality play and experimentation, including touching for pleasure, continue into childhood as a normal, healthy aspect of development. Most adults have some memories of their own childhood play involving touching their bodies or the bodies of other children.

Sexuality development unfolds in a relatively predictable progression during the period between birth and kindergarten (Chrisman & Couchenour 2002, 2004; Honig 2000). Infants and toddlers explore their body parts, including their genitals; begin to develop positive or negative attitudes about their bodies; and experience genital pleasure. Preschoolers and kindergartners may engage in various forms of sexuality-related play, such as undressing to see each other's bodies or playing Doctor, or Mommy and Daddy. They enjoy bathroom humor and will use sexual slang they've heard instead of the proper terms when discussing their body parts. Children at this age show a lot of interest in pregnancy and birth. And they will masturbate at home and sometimes at school. They may show other children their private body parts, try to look at the bodies of other children, and show interest in the bodies of their family members, especially a same-sex parent.

What is important is that teachers and families treat children's sexuality experimentation and play as normal. When a child is found to be engaging in such activity, this is an opportunity to reinforce an important message: That all children experiment this way sometimes; and that such experimenting is alright, just something done in private. How that message is conveyed will vary depending on the child's age and developmental stage. A teacher might ignore or redirect an infant or toddler's sexuality activity, but she might also talk with an older child about its appropriateness in various settings. Children should never be teased, shamed, or punished for self-discovery. If they are, they may begin to hide their activity, and secrecy is always undesirable. Also, giving children the idea that healthy sexuality is "bad" could negatively affect their enjoyment of sex as adults and discourage proper sexual health care (Child & Family Canada 2000).

While healthy adult sexuality is typically deliberate and private, young children are spontaneous and open (Chrisman & Couchenour 2002)—which is why it seems fine to a preschooler to pull down his pants and announce, "I'm a boy, and I have a pee-pee" in the grocery store. Young children usually make no attempt to hide their experimentation (Rothbaum, Grauer, & Rubin 1997). As in all domains, young children learn from their experiences. To young children, experimenting with their developing sexuality is not so different from experimenting with mixing paint or pouring rice through a funnel. However, the time a child spends in sexuality experimentation should not be excessive relative to time spent in other types of experiential learning. (For more signs of possible concern, see the box opposite.)

Experts in sexuality education believe strongly that parents are children's most important sex educators (SIECUS 1998). But so many young children are in child care and other out-of-home settings for much of their day that teachers must share that role in partnership with parents. It is part of every early childhood educator's duty to take into account in her practice what children

Sexuality Behavior That Raises Questions

Sexuality play and experimentation, beginning in infancy and continuing into childhood, are normal, healthy aspects of development. But sometimes a child's sexuality behavior is or becomes unhealthy or inappropriate in some way. Such behavior can even be an indicator of possible sexual abuse. Children's caregivers and teachers should always be sensitive to sexuality behavior that seems inappropriate or atypical for a particular child or for children of a particular age.

How does a teacher establish what is "typical"? First, caregivers should fully understand the natural progression of age-appropriate sexuality play and development. They also should know something about what is typical for children of various cultures or backgrounds. To know whether a particular child is, for example, unusually preoccupied with body parts, teachers must notice how much time the child usually spends in appropriate sexuality play and experimentation and then consider whether the amount or character of the play has changed.

Some uncommon or atypical behaviors that should always cause adults to take note:

• discussions by a child about sexual acts or attempts by a child to engage in a sex act with another child (Tabachnick 2003)

• attempts to engage a stranger in sexuality play

• classmates begin to complain about the child's sexuality play

• unusually detailed or suddenly heightened interest or information about sexual behavior

• inappropriate sexuality play such as use of force, penetration of any body orifice with a foreign object, or attempts to engage a much older or younger child in sexual interaction (Rothbaum, Grauer, & Rubin 1997)

Another problem is hiding or denying or becoming angry when observed engaged in sexuality play. Even once children begin to understand that some body parts and activities are "private," their healthy sexuality play is not fraught with secrecy typically. So although children may hide or deny their behavior if they have been shamed or punished for it, there could be other, more dangerous causes—such as child sexual abuse.

need for healthy sexuality development. This attitude shows respect and nurturing for the development of the whole child and also serves to lessen the risk factors (low self-esteem, secrecy) for abuse in that child's life. (For more about abuse prevention, see **Chapter Five** and **Appendix A.**)

Body ownership

As children become aware of what types of touch from others they enjoy and what makes them uncomfortable, they are beginning to develop the concept of *body ownership*—that they have an inherent right to control when, where, and how they are touched. Likewise, they can begin learning that everyone else shares this same right, and they should respect those wishes in how they touch other people.

The message of body ownership is that children have a right both to reject unwanted contact and to seek affirming touch. Without an understanding of this concept, children may struggle with social skills, and they are left particularly vulnerable to abuse (Elliott 1995; Kaufman et al. 1998). Without a strong sense of body ownership, children do not know how to respond to the experience of uncomfortable, harmful, or abusive touch. Having that sense allows children to recognize when touch may have been inappropriate or abusive, so they can report this touch to a trusted caregiver or parent.

An important corollary to a child's developing a sense of body ownership is for the people around the child, especially the adults, to understand and accept that they do not have the right to touch the child at will. Many adults, especially within families, have been brought up to feel entitled to touch a child whenever and however they want, but this view is at odds with what is best for children themselves.

We must learn to recognize and respect whatever distance the child has chosen to put between us. We do not have the right to move into her or his life space without permission. Children want the right to refuse, to set terms on which at any moment the relationship will proceed. (John Holt, quoted in Lawson 1998)

In the early childhood setting, then, a teacher should have solid reasons for being confident the child will welcome a touch before giving it. Asking and getting the child's permission before touching is one way to assess how the child would feel about it, especially when the child and teacher don't yet know and trust each other. Once a teacher or caregiver has developed a relationship with a child, however, some of the concerns that would apply earlier in their acquaintance no longer arise. When a relationship exists, the child has a level of trust and comfort with the adult. Moreover, the teacher knows the child's touch preferences.

In the situations in which asking permission is called for, the experience of being asked and responding emphasizes body ownership and gives children practice in the giving or declining of permission. And teachers should always respect those preferences if the child's answer is no. In situations that would call for seeking permission to touch if the child were older and able to answer (e.g., before wiping a child's mouth), the caregiver still can show respect for the child's body ownership: She makes sure the child is aware that he is going to be touched and why ("I'm going to clean your face with this wet cloth now") and stops immediately if the child shows any signs of discomfort.

Of course, when a child's safety or health is endangered or when a child needs first aid, seeking permission is unnecessary; in such situations, the teacher would, again, simply make sure the child knows when and why he is being touched, and then do so. For example, if a child falls off of a piece of climbing equipment into a pile of wood mulch, some pieces might have scratched the child's upper legs and genitals. The teacher would tell the child, "To make sure you're not hurt, I need to look at parts of your body under your clothes." Having another teacher or an administrator present at such a time can make both teacher and child feel more comfortable.

Body ownership for infants and toddlers

Learning the concept of body ownership begins shortly after birth when people begin to touch the infant. Teaching the idea is simple at this stage: The caregiver simply tells the child that she is going to touch him and why. For example, when reaching into a crib to pick up a baby, the caregiver would say, "I am going to pick you up and hold you close." Even though the child doesn't understand the words, he gets a sense of being approached in a way that respects him and the interaction, rather than being treated like an object. Then, the caregiver responds to cues that the baby is or is not comfortable with being touched (Honig 2004). Smiles, wiggles, and waving arms would signal the child's desire for and acceptance of the touch; frowning, squirming, pushing away, and crying would indicate rejection of it or discomfort.

The lesson the teacher seeks to communicate to the child is that his comfort is paramount and that for him to express his own body comfort preferences is not only allowed but encouraged. Once, upon being offered a chance to hold a baby in a program she was visiting, Magda Gerber countered, "Do you think the baby would like to be held?" (South Carolina Educational Television 1984). Children may not want to be picked up by strange adults, even if the adults want to.

Some caregivers might feel uneasy or hesitant to talk this way with very young children. It may seem silly or unimportant. But these positive messages not only increase the child's body awareness and sense of body ownership; they also promote language learning (Hart & Risley 1995).

Essential Touch

The nonverbal messages we give infants about their bodies and their individual levels of comfort are also significant. Each time we scrunch up our nose at a dirty diaper, are we communicating distaste or disgust that the baby might read as disgust toward him? Nonverbal expressions about a child's body need to stay as positive as the spoken ones.

Body ownership for preschoolers

During the preschool years, children become more discriminating about what types of touches they find acceptable. Children should have options when games and activities require touching and they don't feel like it. When possible, children shouldn't be forced to hold each other's hands during an activity, for example; instead, a teacher can give a child choices of acceptable alternatives if holding hands feels uncomfortable. If a music and movement activity, for example, typically requires hand-holding, children could be told to "hold hands, fingers, or wrists." Children should be helped to learn how to express their individual preferences. One child might need to learn how to say, "I don't like holding hands" or "Can you hold my fingers?" Another might prefer, "Please let go." Each child should be allowed to determine the amount and kind of touch that personally feels the most comfortable and the least intrusive.

An important exercise for promoting children's understanding of touch is the **Personal Bubble** exercise (Adams & Fay 1981; Hart-Rossi 1984), described in the box in **Chapter Three**. Through this type of personal-space exercise, older preschoolers (as well as older children and adults) can define their individual comfort zones as well as safely explore what it feels like when comfort turns to discomfort. It is also an opportunity to gain and practice the language children need to communicate that discomfort. It is important for children to have the words to let someone know when touch no longer feels comfortable or comforting.

Helping children to understand their individual comfort levels with touch and physical boundaries is critical, and providing language and nonverbal cues to adequately express these comfort levels and body boundaries is imperative. Building a "touch language" or "touch code" for activities focusing on touch is useful. Teachers can help children learn and practice phrases such as, "I don't want a hug, but you can shake my hand" or "Please hug me from the side." Children might want to say, "I don't want a hug, but you can sit beside me" or "Please don't touch my face." Teachers can also model nonverbal cues that express discomfort, such as folding arms across the chest or holding a hand out to say stop.

Children also benefit from learning how to invite positive touch. Teachers might help them say things such as, "Can I have a hug?" or "Will you pat my back?" or "Can I sit with you?" As important as it is for children to learn how to recognize and report inappropriate and abusive touch, it is equally critical that they recognize the need for appropriate and affirming touch and learn how to seek and accept

Essential Touch

it. Through the use of the activities and ideas presented here, children will have opportunities to define what feels good and what feels uncomfortable. Providing the words and the cues to describe these feelings will aid children in seeking out the types of touches they need and prefer.

Teaching children such responses and strategies might seem unnecessary, but fostering body awareness from birth, modeling and teaching language accompanying positive touch, and teaching children how to exercise their right to refuse unwanted or uncomfortable touch will aid children throughout their lives.

Chapter 5

Concerns about Touch in Early Childhood Settings

While I worked toward my undergraduate degree in elementary education, I worked in a preschool setting—first as a teacher's aide, and then as a credentialed lead teacher. [Later, when I looked for a preschool position] I mistakenly assumed that it would be fairly easy to obtain employment. What I overlooked was that in the intervening decade, the child abuse scandals of the 1980s had transpired, in which some, though not all, of the perpetrators had been men. The result was, it seemed, a suspicion of any male who presented himself as an applicant in the early childhood setting. I was amazed that I had to apply at some 15 or 20 locations before I was finally hired. To this day, the interviews of that period are the only unsuccessful job interviews I have ever had.

—A male teacher, now in a fifth grade classroom

Despite evidence of the beneficial effects of positive, nurturing touch in the early years, children are often denied this type of interaction in care and education settings. Why are children deprived of the touch they need to thrive and grow? Sometimes it's out of ignorance—that is, parents or caregivers just don't understand how essential touch is. Sometimes it's family preferences ("Men in our family don't hug") or cultural prohibitions ("Contact between the sexes is against our beliefs"). Sometimes a parent is worried that their very young child will become too attached to the caregiver ("I think Marissa loves Miss Davis more than she does me!"). Sometimes it's personality ("I'm just not a touchy-feely person").

But in today's child care and education context, the answer lies principally in the fear of child sexual abuse. As a whole, educators are professionals who choose the field out of a love for and a need to help and support children. Today, however, many are uneasy about allowing touch in early childhood education settings for fear of somehow enabling potential abusers. They worry, too, about the risk of a staff member being falsely accused, and they seek to remove any possibility of this by eliminating virtually all touch. This is especially true for men. In fact, fear of abuse allegations ranked among the top three reasons men listed in one survey as keeping them from entering the education field (Nelson 2002; Rice & Goessling 2005).

Sadly, sexual abuse of children does occur, although data is understandably hard to collect. Data also varies depending on the definition of *child sexual abuse* used. One common definition is indecent exposure, fondling, genital or oral stimulation, or sexual intercourse (including rape and incest) with a child by an adult or older child for the purpose of sexual gratification. Some also consider placing a child in a situation with a sexual context as abuse. (For more definitions, see **Appendix A.**) Depending on the definition, then, estimates of sexual abuse range between 8% and 14% for boys and between 7% and 32% for girls (Briere & Elliot 2003; Putnam 2003). In one study of substantiated cases of sexual abuse, 30% involved children younger than age 8 (U.S. Department of Health and Human Services 2006). About 85% of victims know their abuser (Oesterreich & Shirer 1994; Telljohann, Everett, & Price 1997). The perpetrator is most likely a family member, neighbor, or friend of the family. As many as 50% of sexual abusers of children are themselves younger than age 18 (Hunter et al. 2003).

But, according to government statistics for 2004, only about 1.2% of the nation's 73.3 million children ages 0–18 years were involved in an abuse investigation; of those only 9.4% involved allegations of sexual abuse. Of the sexual abuse allegations, fewer than 1% were substantiated and involved a "child daycare provider" (U.S. Department of Health and Human Services 2006)—or just 0.001128% of all children. Even considering only data on children (ages 0–18 years) who actually were sexually abused, only 2.3% of the time was the abuser a "child daycare provider"; 63% of abusers were parents or other family members (U.S. Department of Health and Human Services 2006). So, while we cannot say that abuse of young children by early childhood staff *never* happens, it is exceedingly rare—and our child care practices and policies should reflect that rarity. Ignorance and fear should not be allowed to dictate educators' physical interactions with young children. Once we understand that appropriate guidelines and policies can help protect both children and staff, we can avoid overreactions such as "no-touch" rules and return to confidently giving children the nurturing and supportive physical contact they need.

Misguided no-touch policies?

When touch is barred from or minimized in early childhood programs as a result of explicit or implicit policies, it is usually with the intention of protecting both children and staff. Prior to the 1980s, no-touch policies in educational settings were uncommon; but that changed with the widely publicized child sexual abuse cases of that era. As a result, educators began to fear that touches might be misconstrued as sexual in nature. Many programs, and indeed entire school systems, developed no-touch policies (Anderson 2000; Del Prete 1998; Farquhar 2001; Mazur & Pekor 1985).

Where no-touch policies exist, staff—and *male* caregivers and teachers even more often—are instructed to avoid physical contact with the children in their care in virtually all circumstances. Staff members are allowed to touch only to diaper and cleanse younger children, or to restrain children at risk of harming themselves or another child. In all other circumstances, programs with no-touch policies discourage physical contact between staff and children—no patting, no hugging, no cuddling, no rough-and-tumble play.

Sometimes touch is not entirely forbidden, but it is still highly regulated. In such settings, teachers might, for example, be encouraged to hug only from the side instead of from the front, or to offer a high five instead. Another variation is the "professionalization" of touch. In Great Britain and Sweden, for example, trained massage therapists may conduct formal massage sessions in schools and child care programs, while teachers and caregivers often are forbidden by no-touch policies from all physical contact with the children (Appleton 2005).

To have an impact, no-touch policies do not have to exist in writing, although some certainly do. Implicit policies can be just as restrictive. For example, when a female teacher looks with concern at a male colleague about to hug a crying child, she sends him an implicit no-touch message. Even in some early education settings that acknowledge the value of positive touch in theory, actual practices may subtly enforce restrictions based on a child's age or gender, or based on the gender of the teacher.

Leaders in the early childhood education field strongly believe that no-touch policies are not a preferable course of action. The NAEYC position statement *Prevention of Child Abuse in Early Childhood Programs and the Responsibilities of Early Childhood Professionals to Prevent Child Abuse* specifically states in guideline 6:

> **Programs should *not* institute "no-touch policies" to reduce the risk of abuse.** In the wake of well-publicized allegations of child abuse in out-of-home settings and increased concerns regarding liability,

some programs have instituted such policies, either explicitly or implicitly. No-touch policies are misguided efforts that fail to recognize the importance of touch to children's healthy development.... [Instead,] careful, open communication between the program and families about the value of touch in children's development can help to achieve consensus as to acceptable ways for adults to show their respect and support for children in the program. (NAEYC 1996: 2)

Most educators are well aware that children need touch in their lives. But many feel they must comply with no-touch policies, and some even agree with them. As one teacher stated, "I know children need touch, and my instinct is to touch. [But] I think it's better to never touch because you just never know what a student might think or do" (Anderson 2000: 24).

No-touch rules, however, do little to solve the larger society-wide problem of sexual abuse of children.

The reality, which we know but actively ignore, is that these [no-touch policy] measures . . . will have virtually no impact on child abuse. We are unwilling or unable as a society to confront sexual abuse within families, where it is epidemic, so instead we try to impose draconian measures in preschool settings, where proven cases of sexual abuse are rare. (Tobin 1997: 8)

Practices and policies that keep caregivers from giving young children positive, nurturing touch arguably not only fail to prevent abuse but may actually make it more likely. Abuse prevention professionals have identified characteristics in children that make them particularly vulnerable to sexual abuse—including low self-esteem, confusion about what constitutes appropriate touch, and uncertainty about how to question adult authority (Elliott 1995; Kaufman et al. 1998). When positive, nurturing touch and learning about it are lacking, young children miss out on things that might very well have made them safer from potential abusers. An early childhood setting that includes such touch makes children feel secure and loved; it also provides them with experience of what appropriate touch is like and practice at setting boundaries.

Policies to protect children and teachers

If a no-touch policy is not the developmentally appropriate solution to preventing child sexual abuse, what is?

By offering policies and guidance on touch and its implementation, early childhood programs can allow and encourage touch *and* provide protection for children and staff members (Chrisman & Couchenour 2004; Farquhar 2005; Reilly & Martin 1995; Shakeshaft 2004; Strickland & Reynolds 1988). Programs with guidelines on how to use touch face far fewer allegations of child sexual abuse than do programs with little or no guidance surrounding the use of touch (Shakeshaft & Cohan 1995). Programs should include policies and practices that:

Increase the use of positive touch through:

• Staff training in what constitutes appropriate touch; how to incorporate appropriate touch in classroom practice; and general principles of healthy sexuality development

• Education for children about appropriate touch

Confront the possibility of abuse by providing:

• Staff training in what constitutes sexual abuse and suspicion of abuse, mandatory reporting of child abuse, and how to report it

• Program and environmental safeguards, including child supervision ratios and pre-employment checks

• Education for children about what constitutes sexually abusive touch, and how to tell someone

Partner with families by providing:

• Education for families on what constitutes appropriate touch versus sexually abusive touch

• Notice to families regarding the policies and staff training in place to protect children, when staff may use touch for restraint, and how a parent or guardian can lodge a complaint if he or she believes touch has been used inappropriately

---

Accreditation Criteria Address Abuse Issues

The NAEYC Academy for Early Childhood Program Accreditation administers a national, voluntary accreditation system to help raise the quality of all types of preschools, kindergartens, and child care centers. NAEYC Accreditation provides a powerful tool through which early childhood professionals, families, and others concerned about the quality of early childhood education can evaluate programs, compare them with professional standards, strengthen the program, and commit to ongoing evaluation and improvement.

Among the criteria used to accredit programs are two that address child sexual abuse issues (NAEYC 2005b):

Leadership and Management: Health, Nutrition, and Safety Policies and Procedures

10.D.03. The program has a written policy for reporting child abuse and neglect as well as procedures in place that comply with applicable federal, state, and local laws. The policy includes requirements for staff to report all suspected incidents of child abuse, neglect, or both by families, staff, volunteers, or others to the appropriate local agencies. Staff who report suspicions of child abuse or neglect where they work are immune from discharge, retaliation, or other disciplinary action for that reason alone unless it is proven that the report is malicious.

10.D.04. The program has written procedures to be followed if a staff member is accused of abuse or neglect of a child in the program that protect the rights of the accused staff person as well as protect the children in the program.

For more about NAEYC Accreditation, visit www.naeyc.org/accreditation/academy.asp.

• An open-door policy that encourages family members to drop in on the program unannounced at any time

Proactive policy specifics

Without appropriate guidance, teachers often feel forced to withhold touch, or they develop their own personal policies of how, when, and where to touch children (Piper & Smith 2003). It is better for children when programs proactively develop and implement a set of strong, supportive guidelines. With such guidelines in place, programs can offer touch without fear of harming children, and staff have a context for discussing their goals and concerns. (See the box **Questions to Talk Over in Your Program** in **Chapter Three.**)

When thinking about, developing, and implementing touch policies, programs should avoid phrasing them as rules that *forbid* or *prohibit*. Instead, we should think of such policies as guidance that can *encourage* and *allow*. Policies should stipulate how to offer touch, how to teach children about appropriate and inappropriate touch, how to structure classroom environments and activities to include touch without compromising children's safety, and how to recognize indicators in children that abusive touch might have occurred. (See the **Appendix** for sample language and other material pertinent to many of the policies described below.)

Body ownership. Sexual abuse prevention policies should establish certain baseline understandings. Prime among these is children's ultimate right to control when, where, and how they are touched. Policies should define how children will be taught the concept of body ownership. They should address a child's right to "adequate supervision" when vulnerable body parts are being touched, such as during diapering. Adequate supervision might mean that more than one adult must be present when a child's vulnerable body parts are touched or that cameras record the interaction, as protection for both caregiver and child. Adequate supervision might also mean that only staff members well-trained in caring for infants and toddlers may perform the functions that involve such touch.

Policies should address the child's right to decline being touched by an adult and how situational factors (e.g., presence of a parent or other staff member; length of the relationship with the child) influence the ways teachers should approach touch with children. When a relationship exists, the child has a level of trust and comfort with the adult, and casual touches such as a hand on the shoulder or arm may be okay without asking beforehand. Moreover, the teacher knows more about the child's touch preferences—e.g., that it is okay to put a hand on Jaime's or Martin's shoulder, while this gesture is unwelcome to Elissa.

There are exceptions that policies also should address. Even on the first day a child is in the room, a teacher should not hesitate to touch for reasons of safety, such as grabbing a child before she runs in front of a car; to assess an injury and administer first aid; or to use temporary restraint to protect a child from hurting himself or others. When the teacher needs to touch a child for any of these reasons, the best course is for a second teacher to be present, if possible. Also, the child's parents or guardian should be notified immediately afterward. If a second teacher is not available, some type of follow-up, such as a written memorandum for the record, would assist the teacher in explaining the facts.

Teachers should find in program policies guidance on how to include appropriate touch without compromising children's safety. The National Network for Child Care (Reilly & Martin 1995) offers this sample policy language:

> Be aware of children's personal boundaries and respect them. For example, some people like being close and getting and giving hugs. Others don't like a lot of close contact. Sometimes we forget that children have those preferences, too.

And this:

> Hugs are okay if they are appropriate and if both people are comfortable with them. Take your cues from the child's body language or simply ask, "Is it okay if I hug you?" If you don't feel comfortable with a hug from a child, tell her [or him] in a gentle way. Then suggest an alternative, such as holding her [his] hand or putting her [his] hand on your shoulder or arm.

Telling and reporting. Program policies must explicitly state that children have the right to tell an adult if they feel a teacher's touch has been inappropriate. To implement such a reporting policy, children, as soon as they are old enough, should be taught to first ask the adult who is engaging in the touch that seems inappropriate or confusing to stop. Then, if the adult persists, the child tells another, trusted grown-up either at the program or at home that an inappropriate touch has occurred.

For infants, toddlers, and preschoolers, adequate supervision is most essential, as these children are too young to report incidents in most cases. For them, the ideal is for a second teacher always to be present, to ensure that touch remains safe and appropriate and to give staff protection against false allegations. The presence of a second adult may not always be possible, but it is safest for both children and staff. Video cameras or wide viewing windows into classrooms in lieu of a second teacher can be beneficial, too.

Teachers and other staff must be very clear about their mandated responsibility to report incidents or suspicions of abuse. Policies should include guidance about whether that legal mandate is met in their specific state if the teacher reports to a third party (e.g., parent or center director) instead of directly to a law enforcement authority or child protection agency.

Structural and environmental factors. Effective sexual abuse prevention policies also protect children *and* staff members by addressing structural and environmental issues. An important step is setting an open-door policy that encourages families to drop in unannounced whenever possible. Continuous and open access for families to all parts of the early childhood program (Reilly & Martin 1995) helps safeguard children. To aid in visual supervision, a program might install observation booths overlooking each room, window panels in doors, half-doors, or video cameras. With windows between classrooms, no teacher is left alone with a child, and teachers can give each other support.

Having more than one adult always present with children can offer additional protection for children and teachers. When this level of staffing is not possible, a program could try grouping children of similar ages and developmental levels so that staff members can support each other, or placing groups with only one teacher in the most visible classroom areas.

Finally, effective program policies include certain pre-employment requirements for staff. Among these requirements are a satisfactory result on a criminal record check, carefully documented references from past employers, and statements about the candidate's ability to work satisfactorily with children. These should include a signed statement from the candidate that she or he has never been found by credible evidence to be guilty of causing physical, emotional, or sexual harm to a child.

Dissemination and implementation

Having clear, effective, and written staff policies governing the use of touch in an early childhood program is important. A copy of these policies should be offered to families. Families are more likely to be supportive if they know and understand a program's policies, so including them in a family handbook can be beneficial. Information about a program's touch policies should be a regular part of each orientation for new families, as well. Involving families in discussion of the need all children have for positive touch is important in balancing concerns that may make them overly fearful of abuse.

Perhaps most important to remember is that program policies—no matter how well written and disseminated—are only effective if they are implemented properly and consistently. To ensure that staff members understand and follow the program's policies, training on those policies should be included as a part of each orientation for new employees and annually thereafter in inservice workshops.

Again, to help families understand all aspects of this complex issue, they could be invited to attend some of the training sessions, or separate workshops could be developed just for them. (Outlines of sample training sessions suitable for staff, families, and both are provided in **Appendix D.**) Education—in the form of written policies and live training sessions—is key to helping families understand both the essential importance of touch for their children and also the ways in which a program offers touch while safeguarding the children in its care.

Effective abuse prevention programs

As sexual abuse cases have become more highly publicized, many educators have worked to develop programs aimed at educating children in an effort to prevent sexual abuse (Bolen 2003; Plummer [1993] 2005). Preschoolers and kindergartners have been shown to respond to prevention programs as well as or better than first- and second-graders (Davis & Gidyez 2000; Kraizer, Witte, & Fryer 1989). Most prevention programs begin in first or second grade, but the responsiveness of younger children coupled with the significant percentage of abuse that occurs before age 8 suggests that prevention programs can be useful with these children.

Prevention programs should be tailored to the age and developmental stage of the children. The American Academy of Pediatrics (2000) recommends the following guidelines:

- 18 months—Teach the proper names for body parts.

• 3 to 5 years old—Teach about the "private parts" of the body (those a swimsuit covers) and how to say no to [unwanted touches or sexual advances]. Give straightforward answers about sex.

• 5 to 8 years old—Discuss safety away from home and school; develop the idea of inappropriate touch (of the private parts) versus appropriate touch. Encourage children to talk about scary experiences.

Encouraging discussion shows children that sexuality is nothing to be ashamed of. Eliminating secrecy greatly reduces the threat of sexual abuse.

Children must have the knowledge and skills needed to defend against abusive approaches, and be able to successfully apply them should the need arise, before the abuse occurs (Bolen 2003). That does not mean prevention programs should provide explicit information about abuse that might frighten children and suggest that the adults they love might harm them (Kraizer, Witte, & Fryer 1989). Instead, programs should foster children's self-esteem and social skills, help children experience and learn about appropriate touch, and offer instruction on how to say no to authority figures—in particular how to decline unwanted and harmful contact (Elliott 1995; Kaufman et al. 1998).

Fostering children's social and emotional development is part of any good early childhood program. Teachers foster self-esteem when they provide safe and caring environments for children, environments that meet both social and safety needs. For example, a child new to a program feels safe when provided comfort during naptime in a new place. That comfort may come from a kind word, a quiet story together, or a soothing backrub. But teaching children to distinguish inappropriate touch *and* to say no offers special challenges.

Helping children distinguish inappropriate touch

One challenge particular to sexual abuse prevention programs is helping children establish a context of *appropriate versus inappropriate* touch. Unfortunately, many programs have proved ineffective and insufficient in this regard

(Carlson 2003). Research conducted with pre- and post-tests as part of one sexual abuse prevention program with school-age children concluded that they "did not make gains on a number of difficult concepts (like good versus bad touch) even after participating in the prevention program" (Tutty 2000: 287). In a review of another school-age prevention program, participating children did not score significantly higher than children who had no experience with prevention training (Gilbert 1994).

For a prevention program to actually be effective, children must come to understand the difference between appropriate and inappropriate touch, because most sexual abuse begins as nonthreatening, nonabusive physical contact between the child and a person the child knows and often trusts. This contact might be accompanied by loving words and assurances of care by the perpetrator. Because this initial touch does not feel "bad" to the child, children often do not recognize it as inappropriate (Casper 1999; Gilbert 1994; Tutty 2000).

Successful abuse prevention programs share components that help children learn to distinguish between appropriate and inappropriate touch. In one example (Carlson 2003), presentation of the concept of appropriate and inappropriate touch—as plotted on a Touch Continuum—with role-play, puppets, and video representations in short intervals (up to 20 minutes), repeated several times in a row over a period of weeks, resulted in a clearer understanding of this concept. (For more on the Touch Continuum, see the box on pages 72–73.) Children's physical involvement in learning has also been found to improve program success (Davis & Gidyez 2000):

> Physical participation may have some advantage over verbal participation in teaching prevention skills to children due to their stage of cognitive development. Children have difficulty using symbolic representations in abstract thought; thus they are less able to logically think through hypothetical situations. Physical involvement makes the information and skills being taught more concrete and salient for the children. (262)

Physical participation might be children using role-play, perhaps to practice identifying an unwanted hug from Aunt Ethel as "inappropriate." The rehearsing and the time spent in role-play are significant in leading to greater gains for children in child abuse prevention education.

In addition, children must first be able to comprehend the concept of touch as appropriate or inappropriate, *then* understand that sexual abuse occurs when an adult or older child touches them inappropriately (Pinon, Hulsey, & Woodland 1999). But without exposure to appropriate touch, children have enormous difficulty in determining what constitutes inappropriate touch. Programs need to instruct children about how touch feels on an individual basis, so that each child can develop some context of appropriate versus inappropriate touch. Tickling, a hug, a backrub, for example—all can be appropriate, but can also be intrusive and potentially abusive for a child who finds any of them threatening or unpleasant. Teachers must determine child by child what touch is okay and what touch is problematic, then proceed from that place. All these elements viewed together bring us back to the essential role of positive, nurturing touch in the early childhood education context.

What works. It is important for educators to articulate clear safety guidelines to children instead of only encouraging to them to use their feelings to interpret touch—because some appropriate touches can feel "bad" (e.g., getting a shot at the doctor) and some inappropriate touches can feel "good" (e.g., Cousin Hank putting his hands inside your shirt to rub your back). Children taught safety guidelines (e.g., "It is not okay for an older child to touch or look at your private parts") show more ability to recognize unsafe situations than do children taught only to use their instincts. Child predators often begin a process of grooming a child for abuse by giving gifts, special privileges, and touch that is not inappropriate, all of which the child might well enjoy (Child & Family Canada 2000).

The Touch Continuum

The Touch Continuum was proposed by child abuse prevention educator Cordelia Anderson (2000) to "help ensure that touch was talked about in a balanced manner within our broader child sexual abuse prevention curriculum" (25). In a Touch Continuum discussion, the teacher leads the children (preschoolers or older) to characterize three categories of touch and to place, from their own perspective, where various types of touch fit into those categories.

Three categories of touch

1. Nurturing. Touch that *feels good and is positive*—children typically call this "good" touch and mention hugs from family members, petting animals, holding hands with friends

2. Confusing. Touch that feels *confusing*—children typically mention hugs that are too tight, or hugs from someone unfamiliar. Confusing touch can be:

- Touch that is good but feels bad—e.g., a shot at the doctor's office
- Touch that feels good but is harmful—e.g., inappropriate sexual touch

Other factors that can make touch confusing are:

- It is not clearly positive or negative
- The intent of the giver is not clear
- The receiver does not understand or misinterprets the intent of the giver
- The receiver is not used to being touched in this particular way
- What the person is saying is different from what his or her hands are doing (i.e., the verbal and physical messages are not the same)
- The giver or the receiver is used to equating all physical contact with sex
- It feels good but it is shrouded in secrecy or shame
- It is in conflict with the attitudes, values, or morals of the giver, the receiver, or both
- It does not fit within the context of the relationship of the giver to the receiver (e.g., it is either too intimate or too formal)

- The receiver does not like the contact or is uncomfortable with it even though it is okay or not a secret

3. **Exploitative.** Touch that is *harmful and abusive*—children typically call this "bad" touch and mention being hit, slapped, kicked, bullied. Exploitative touch is manipulative or forced; it is touch that hurts but has no beneficial purpose (unlike that shot at the doctor's office).

Lack of touch is on both ends of the continuum. It is "good" when it results from putting limits on the type of touch we want to receive. It is "bad" when it results in severe deprivation. As discussed in **Chapter Two,** such deprivation can, like abusive touch, have very negative consequences.

Using the continuum

Talking about "confusing" touch can help children know they can speak up or ask questions when they are uncertain about a type of touch. Touch is often as confusing for adults as it is for children. We all need to understand that we should stop if we are touching someone in a way that he or she does not like or finds confusing. Through the conversation about all three types of touch, teachers also should reinforce to children that they have the power to set boundaries around the types of touch they find confusing, harmful, or both.

The Touch Continuum, then, is a tool to help children "develop skills to ask for the touch they want, to talk about the touch that confuses them, and to do what they can to refuse or set limits concerning the touch they do not like" (Anderson 2000: 25).

Adapted with permission from C. Anderson (2000, October/November), The touch continuum: Part of a risk-reduction curriculum, *SIECUS Report* 29 (1): 24–27.

Author's note: For children too young to have an abstract discussion, teachers instead can role-play with other teachers or introduce pictures that depict the three categories of touches, so that children can increase their awareness and begin to learn the language of touch. Children's videos designed specifically to teach sexual abuse prevention strategies have been effective. Picture books would be appropriate here, too.

Educators should also be careful about how they present these safety guidelines and not label all sexual or genital touch as bad. Labeling all such touch as bad can hinder children's healthy sexuality development and general sexual healthcare. It also creates confusion and misplaced guilt for some children who have been sexually abused. Because the touch of sexual abuse can create confused feelings in children and may also be accompanied by things that can feel good (e.g., loving words, gifts), abused children may misconstrue messages of "bad touch" to mean there is something bad about them for being involved (Child & Family Canada 2000).

Helping children set boundaries and say no

The second challenge of abuse prevention is ensuring that the child will say no to an offending adult and will report unwanted touch to another, trusted adult. For the most part, prevention programs have addressed only children's confusion about what constitutes appropriate touch (Casper 1999; Gilbert 1994; Tutty 2000). They usually do not adequately address self-esteem development or offer information about how children can question adult authority when their bodies are involved.

Expecting a child, especially a young one, to stand up against an adult or older child *just because we tell her to* is probably unrealistic. The typical young child inherently sees such people as more powerful and would be inclined naturally to obey being told, "Come with me" or "Don't tell anyone our secret." They may even have been explicitly taught to, as this researcher found:

> Many of the prevention concepts that make up child abuse programs are not [facts] but beliefs, some of which contradict cultural and family norms about how children should behave. For example, the concept that gives children permission to "sometimes say no to a grown-up" is contrary to what many children have been taught. (Tutty 2000: 276)

And telling another trusted adult about an incident can seem to contradict other messages the child may have received, such as "no one likes a tattle-tale."

Children seem to best learn to say no to harmful touch from programs in which they actively *practice* saying no to authority figures. Physical participation in role-play gives children a model of what action to take when con-

---

Talking to Young Children about Inappropriate Touch

It can be hard to know what to say to young children about inappropriate touch. The following sample text may give you an idea of how to start a conversation about the subject:

> Sometimes when you are at school, our teachers will talk to you about touch. Sometimes they will want to touch you. A teacher might touch you on the back or shoulder when you arrive in the morning. She might give you a hug if you need one. Or she might ask if you would like a back rub at naptime. These are all ways we show we care about you. These are good kinds of touches.
>
> But maybe you don't feel like a hug or a pat on the back. If you don't, you can say no to the teacher. You are in charge of your body. When you say no, the teacher will listen. If you say no to a hug or pat or back rub, the teacher will listen and not touch you that way.
>
> *   *   *
>
> Grownups should not touch you in ways that make you feel bad. This is true at school and other places too. You are in charge of your body. You can say no if you don't want to be touched. If you say no, the grownup should not touch you.
>
> What if the grownup still touches you after you say no? What if they touch you in a bad way? As soon as you can, go tell a different grownup. Tell a grownup you trust. You could tell your mother or father. Or tell a teacher here at school.
>
> Tell, even if the grownup who touched you asked you to keep it a secret.

The important points are to be open and honest, use language the child can understand, and revisit the subject over time.

---

fronted with inappropriate touch (Davis & Gidyez 2000; Kraizer, Witte, & Fryer 1989). Because sexual abuse so often begins with nonthreatening touch, children benefit from learning to decline potentially innocent but unwanted touch. During role-play, then, a child might practice saying no to a teacher ruffling his hair or pinching his cheek. He might also practice warding off unwanted touch when the potential abuser adds flattery, emotional coercion, rejection, bribery, or secrecy (Kraizer, Witte, & Fryer 1989). For example, will he continue to avoid a hug when the teacher protests that he must not like her anymore, or when she offers him a new toy in return?

What works. When encouraging children to tell another adult about an incident of unwanted touch, the telling should not be phrased as "tattling"—an act that children may see as bad. Instead, teachers should instruct children to approach a trusted adult for the purpose of asking for help. Also, it is important to reinforce the ideas that adults are responsible for the protection of children, and that children are never at fault in situations of abuse (Child & Family Canada 2000).

Partnerships with families

Families are always important partners in a developmentally appropriate early childhood program—but more so when the topic is child sexual abuse, if only to recognize the reality that abusers are likely to be a family member, neighbor, or friend of the family. Successful prevention programs typically include a family component in addition to classroom instruction (Hart-Rossi 1984; Spungen, Jensen, & Finkelstein 1989; Wilkerson 1994).

Educators of young children can be family educators as well. After their own personal awareness and knowledge have increased, parents will be better able to instruct their children in the concepts of appropriate and inappropriate touch, saying no to authority figures, and reporting to a trusted adult. Parent education also provides a safe venue for families to discuss the complexities of touch in young children's lives without fear or shame. Families aware of the role they play in helping protect their children can work more effectively both to support safe, nurturing touch in early childhood programs and to prevent inappropriate and sexually victimizing touch elsewhere.

After instruction in abuse prevention, families also are better able to respond quickly and effectively to reports of abuse from their own children (Lanning, Ballard, & Robinson 1999; Spungen, Jensen, & Finkelstein 1989). Taking children's reports seriously and responding quickly and effectively is imperative if healing is to take place.

In NAEYC's position statement on preventing child abuse (1996) and its Code of Ethical Conduct (2005a), NAEYC suggests that early childhood programs adopt policies and practices that promote close partnerships with families; provide a variety of supportive services to families; and advocate for children, families, and teachers in community and society. Collaboration between early childhood programs and the families they serve is the best possible way to protect and support children. Nurturing touch is best offered within the context of strong and trusting relationships between adults and children; positive relations between staff and families help foster closeness between staff and children (Baker & Manfredi/Petitt 2004). When families are informed upon entering an early childhood program of the value that program places on touch—and its relation to child sexual abuse prevention—touch can be offered with family awareness, understanding, and support.

Chapter 6

When Children Have Touch-Related Special Needs

I have never felt comfortable touching my mom and dad. Every holiday, my mom always has the same request—a hug from me. I'm still pretty stiff, but I manage 5 or 10 seconds. It sure pleases her. On a rare occasion, I will pat my mom's arm. . . . Also, as a child it was truly unbearable for me to touch or wear clothes made from soft fabrics. I would immediately get a cold, chilled feeling, get goose bumps over my entire body, and my hair would stand up on end! Once, at around age 7, I saw a man in a restaurant wearing a soft, fuzzy sweater and he was gently rubbing up and down his sleeve. I told my parents I couldn't stay in there. Just the sight of someone else touching a soft fabric was intolerable.

—A college student, reflecting on growing up with a sensory integration dysfunction

As **Chapter Two** described, touch has therapeutic benefits for a variety of health conditions. But sometimes the touch itself is a problem. All of us, children included, prefer certain smells, sights, textures, sounds, and we all differ in how well we interact with our physical world. A young child who resists being picked up out of the sandbox, wrinkles her nose at the smell of coffee, holds her pencil funny, doesn't enjoy having her toes tickled, or loves to rock in the rocking chair is developing typically. One who screams whenever his feet leave the ground, cries when water runs in the sink, can't hold a paper cup without crushing it, never makes eye contact, or twirls in place for an hour straight is not interacting with his environment in a typical or healthy manner. At some point an invisible line has been crossed that distinguishes typical individual preferences and differences from conditions that require clinical intervention.

This chapter looks particularly at children with special needs that directly relate to touch and related senses. In spite of our best intentions to provide children with positive touch experiences, for some children touch is uncomfortable, even painful, or it is difficult for them to process. This is sometimes a result of prenatal conditions. Babies who were exposed to alcohol in utero, for example, are often intolerant of touch of any kind (Marcellus 2000). Children may be born with or suffer an injury of the brain or sensory system. Infants who have suffered abuse or neglect can have difficulty accepting touch or may seek touch indiscriminately (see the box opposite).

Sensory integration dysfunction

Sensory integration is a neurobiological process in which the brain analyzes, interprets, and acts on sensory stimulation taken in from the environment (Ayres 2005; Hatch-Rasmussen 1995). Sensory integration handles information from our five classic senses of sight, hearing, smell, taste, and touch, as well as our senses of movement/balance and body position. When a child's brain struggles with sensory information, this condition is referred to as *sensory integration dysfunction*—that is, the child takes in information from the senses in the normal way, but the information is understood and used in an unusual

Indiscriminate Friendliness

In stark contrast to children who avoid touch due to a physical or emotional disorder, some children seek touch in a reckless fashion from virtually anyone. This emotional condition known as *indiscriminate friendliness* occurs when a child has failed to form a secure attachment during infancy and early childhood, typically as a result of neglect, deprivation, and absence of a consistent caregiver (Albus & Dozier 1999; Bower 2000; Chisholm 1998). This touch-related attachment disorder occurs most frequently in institutional settings where nurturing, responsive care or sensory stimulation is severely lacking.

Because these children were unable to form a secure attachment to a primary caregiver at an early age, given the opportunity they may later reach out to anyone they perceive as a possible caregiver figure. Children with this condition will express affection, usually physical, to anyone who is receptive. Such touching behavior seems reckless—even dangerous—as the child tends to solicit and accept physical affection from anyone who offers it, whether that person is harmless or not. The child may be confused about which touching behaviors are appropriate and which are not.

Nurturing touch from a caring adult can help a child with this condition by helping the child to begin building a secure attachment to that caregiver. But this new secure attachment later in childhood cannot replace its lack during infancy and the toddler years. The child's indiscriminate friendliness may decrease; however, it will likely never disappear completely, as no cure for this specific attachment disorder is known (Bower 2000).

way that can cause pain, fear, or confusion (Greenspan 2004; Schaaf & Miller 2005). The child's physical, cognitive, emotional, and social development can be compromised; movement, fine motor and gross motor skills, and social interactions can be difficult or even impossible.

The term sensory integration dysfunction describes two types of problems. One is a problem with *modulation* of sensory information. A child with this type would either be unusually sensitive to the sensory stimulation he encounters and tend to recoil from it (overreactive/hypersensitive) or would not be satisfied with typical sensory stimulation and tend to seek it out in ways that may be dangerous (underreactive/hyposensitive) (Kranowitz 2006). The second kind of sensory integration dysfunction is when the child has difficulty *processing* sensory information. (This child may or may not also have a modulation problem.) Such a child is inefficient at making use of sensory information. She is biologically unable to translate information into action, preventing her from carrying out something she wants to do, such as climbing a step or answering a question (Kranowitz 2006).

Sensory integration dysfunction can be a disorder on its own or it can accompany other neurological conditions such as autism (see the box opposite), dyslexia, multiple sclerosis, and speech delays. Children with sensory integration dysfunction vary individually in which of their senses are affected and to what degree. Children with touch-related special needs have difficulty modulating and processing touch *(tactile)*, movement and balance *(vestibular)*, and body position *(proprioceptive)* information primarily.

Tactile sensation

Tactile sensation is felt and processed by the nerves in the skin and experienced in the brain as touch, temperature, pleasure, pain, and pressure. For a child with tactile dysfunction a hug, for example, that would otherwise feel soothing might feel uncomfortable or painful (hypersensitivity). These children may feel more than typical discomfort from seams or tags in their clothing or from the texture of the fabric. They may be unwilling to get their hands dirty or to put their hands into substances such as shaving cream, sand, or finger paint they find unpleasant. Or, conversely, a hyposensitive child might be unable to process that he is squeezing too tight, making the person he is hugging uncomfortable. Hyposensitive children might experience little

Autism

What is generally referred to as "autism" is actually a range of developmental disorders typically appearing in the early years and varying in type and severity. For this reason, most experts prefer the term *autism spectrum disorder* (sometimes also called pervasive developmental disorder, or PDD), which includes conditions such as Asperger's syndrome, childhood disintegrative disorder, Rett syndrome, and autistic disorder. A recent study estimates that 3.4 of every 1,000 children ages 3–10 have autism (Yeargin-Allsopp et al. 2003).

Children with autism spectrum disorder often have sensory integration disorders. This does not mean, however, that children with sensory integration disorders are necessarily also autistic. Children with autism may also have difficulty with social skills, expressive and receptive language, fine motor and gross motor skills, appropriate behavior, and independent organizational skills (U.S. Government Accountability Office 2005).

The methods identified in this chapter have proved quite successful with autistic children in addressing both their sensory integration and their educational needs. In addition, touch in the form of therapeutic massage results in greater on-task behavior and improvements in sleep patterns for children with autism (Escalona et al. 2001; Field et al. 1997a). They are more attentive in school and show greater social skills both in the classroom and on the playground. When parents use massage therapy at home, they also note improved sleep patterns, reduced stress levels, and more positive social interactions in their autistic children (Cullen & Barlow 2002).

or no pain; or they may move in ways that generate tactile input, such as bumping into others or playing in a rough way.

Sometimes a hypersensitive child—more than just experiencing discomfort—has an extreme aversion to tactile stimulation, a condition often referred to as *tactile defensiveness*. Such a child may run from touch or shut down completely when touched (Cantu 2002). Some children with this processing problem may appear to be hyperactive when, in reality, they are simply overreacting to stimulation. Harmless tactile stimulation may feel threatening, and the child may withdraw from simple touches such as having his nose wiped with a tissue or getting a gentle pat on her back. Although such a child may at times seek physical contact, the contact itself might result in the child pulling away.

Vestibular sensation

The vestibular sense governs balance and monitors movement. Nerves in the inner ear help the brain determine whether the head and body are upright or tilted. When children have a hypersensitive vestibular sense, they may have trouble climbing up or down or traversing uneven or unstable terrain. They tend to move hesitantly or clumsily. They may become dizzy or experience motion sickness easily or become disoriented after bending over. In some children, their discomfort is expressed as fearfulness—e.g., fear of heights or of slides and swings. In contrast, hyposensitive children may feel compelled to move, sometimes excessively, to give their vestibular system input to process because it isn't stimulated by normal levels of movement. For example, they might spend a lot of time whirling, jumping, or spinning.

Proprioceptive sensation

The proprioceptive sense gauges every aspect of the body's position or orientation—even without the use of sight—by using sensory information from nerves in the muscles, joints, and tendons. The proprioceptive sense lets the child know where each part of his body is in space and how it is moving. When this information is integrated in the brain improperly, children must rely on sight alone for their sense of where their body is. They are often unable to sit in a chair without falling out or to step up or down at the curb without tripping. This sense is also essential for the planning and execution of fine motor control, and children with a sensory integration dysfunction in this area may avoid or have trouble performing tasks such as buttoning, writing, or self-feeding. In general, children with an impaired proprioceptive sense may fall easily, appear clumsy or sloppy, and have an odd posture (Hatch-Rasmussen 1995). Hypersensitive children may carry themselves in a stiff and tense manner, while hyposensitive children may slump (Kranowitz 2005).

Identifying and treating children

Many children with sensory integration dysfunctions can learn to better modulate and process the sensory input they receive. Strong family communications are especially vital when children with special needs of any kind are in early childhood programs—and this is true for children with touch disorders, too. Early childhood staff must work together with family members and trained professionals (such as physical therapists, occupational therapists, and child psychologists) to meet each child's needs.

Families are often the first to notice that a child's sensory capabilities aren't functioning normally; sometimes concerns arise during a well-baby checkup at the pediatrician or in routine screening at a school or center. From there, the first step is a comprehensive evaluation and specific diagnosis by a trained occupational therapist or other specialist. Once the problem is properly identified, an individualized treatment plan is designed. The therapist helps the teacher to incorporate specific activities to address the child's special sensory integration needs. These activities require ongoing assessment and supervision by the therapist.

The treatment plan the specialist designs has among its goals to help the child meet the basic human need for a *sensory diet*—that is, the "total balance of sensory input that we need and use every day" to function (Gould & Sullivan 1999: 182). When working normally, our brain automatically and effortlessly prompts us to seek out or create the sensory experiences we need and to handle the ones we encounter, using those sensory inputs to make sense of, learn about, and respond to the world around us. But for a child with problems of sensory integration, inputs that might normally be calming or positive have the opposite effect, and integrating sensory inputs might demand difficult, frustrating, conscious effort that the child's brain can't always translate into well-planned and executed actions. These children need help from their families, teachers, and therapists "to create the 'just right' sensory diet" they need to retrain their brain's sensory integration system (Gould & Sullivan 1999: 182).

A therapeutic sensory diet includes environmental elements, activities, and various sensory stimuli prescribed by the specialist specifically for that child to help her integrate tactile, vestibular, and proprioceptive senses (Nackley 2006). The child might then receive her diet either from the specialist or from her classroom teacher, depending on the individual child and the activities prescribed. For a child diagnosed with a vestibular sensory integration dysfunction, for example, therapy might prescribe a schedule that would have the child rock in a rocking chair, swing, hang upside down, and dance, as well as roll and balance on large, rubber therapy balls. Engaging such a child in movement activities such as swiveling (e.g., in a swivel chair) or spinning (e.g., in a tire swing) and activities where she must close her eyes (e.g., swinging blindfolded at a piñata) also helps stimulate the vestibular sense.

The figure opposite shows additional examples of intervention strategies that might be prescribed as part of a specific sensory diet. While they may look similar, even identical, to activities any classroom teacher might offer, the difference is they are tailored to the child's age and disorder and are performed on a specific schedule toward therapeutic goals.

Specific Intervention Strategies That Might Be Included in a Child's Sensory Diet

Activity	Equipment	Frequency
Tactile *(touch)*		
Discriminatory texture play—child experiences a variety of textures	Feely boxes, hidden objects in a sand box	Several times throughout the day
Vestibular *(movement and balance)*		
Swinging and rocking at different speeds; stopping and starting Moving to music; stopping and starting at a visual or verbal signal	Playground swing, blanket swing, rocking horse, scooter board, balance board, therapy ball Music source	Three to five times daily for about 5 minutes each time
Proprioceptive *(body position and motor control)*		
Pouring—child pours back and forth from container to container "Bulldozer"—one child sits in a large cardboard box while another child pushes him across the floor (Kranowitz 2005)	Containers; variety of sub-stances such as rice, beans, water Cardboard box	Available through-out the day

Creating supportive classrooms

I use touch in many ways while I teach. Sometimes a steady hand to
guide a student who is just beginning to learn how to walk ... other
times, hand-over-hand guidance to teach a new skill. Then there are
times when students need to be held, not only to [help them] calm
themselves down but also to let them know that there is someone who
cares about them. Touch plays such an important role in a special
educator's job; it is the necessary ingredient for a child's first success in
school.

—A special education preschool teacher

In addition to specific intervention strategies, there are some general principles teachers can follow and simple environmental adjustments they can make to help create safe spaces for *all* children, especially those with sensory integration problems. The same modifications made for children with difficulties also support the development of body awareness and individual touch preferences among typically developing children.

For example, a teacher accommodates all children, but especially a child with tactile sensitivities, when he allows the class to define their individual spaces during circle time by sitting on placemats or carpet squares, instead of making them sit in a tight or rigid form. The children place their squares at distances from their classmates that they each find personally comfortable. When the class must line up, the teacher can allow them to form a loose line, instead of making them stand close together. He doesn't require them to hold hands; instead, he lets them hold fingers, a wrist, or simply touch fingertips, and he has them ask first ("May I hold your hand?"). He models being sensitive and respectful of physical cues—such as squirming, moving away from the other child, or pushing and shoving—that indicate another person is feeling uncomfortable.

Supporting with general principles

Showing sensitivity to each child's personal comfort level is one of the general principles for creating "safe" spaces. Here are some others:

Offer a variety of sensory experiences. The sensory inputs that upset one child might have no effect on another. Only by being exposed to different experiences (textures, shapes, movements, orientations) over time can a child determine which are most or least comfortable. In this way, the child can move into play situations after determining an individual comfort level. When children experience touch they find uncomfortable, they have an opportunity to learn how to handle it. In an environment where they feel safe, children will be more likely to push themselves to try materials they initially find uncomfortable, and in some cases, they are able to become relatively comfortable with those materials after they learn how to desensitize themselves to them. Also, when a variety of experiences are offered, chances increase that each child will find a fit with his preferences and sensitivities and so be able to participate in more classroom activities, if in his own way. For example, in a dough activity, a typically developing child might experience cooked dough, bread dough, and shampoo dough by kneading, rolling, and squishing; a child with sensory integration dysfunction might choose to experience only cooked dough and might only punch it with a finger. When teachers offer choices of materials along a continuum to all the children, each child will find an individual comfort level.

Be sensitive to each child's personal comfort levels and abilities. Children should never be forced or pushed beyond their individual level of comfort. Instead, every day they should be provided opportunities and encouraged to try experiences they might not feel comfortable with initially. A teacher should never force a child to finger paint, for example, or to walk barefoot through pine straw or to hold her hands under water, if the sensation would distress the child. (The only time a teacher should ever force an uncomfortable sensory situation is for reasons of safety or health, such as grabbing a child who is averse to being touched who is about to fall.)

For example, children who need a large personal space should always be allowed to bring up the rear of a group. Children who need lots of tactile stimulation should be allowed to have more shaving cream, more dough, more sand, and a larger area in which to work. Children should be able to establish their own comfortable distances between other children at circle time, in lines, at tables. A teacher shouldn't make children hold hands if they don't want to, and certainly shouldn't insist on a naptime back rub for a child who prefers that the teacher just sit on the floor next to his cot.

Let the child know that you are going to touch him and why before you do so. The teacher should give the child time to prepare for touch that the child may find extremely uncomfortable. For example, telling a child, "I see spaghetti sauce still on your arm. I need to wash it off" lets the child know what's coming next and why. Once a teacher is accustomed to the child's touch preferences and responses, so much advance verbal communication may not be necessary. But, then again, overcommunicating is rarely detrimental. A corollary to this is **the child should always be approached from the front,** so the child sees the teacher before she touchs or speaks to him. Unexpectedly tapped on the shoulder from behind, the typical human reaction is to jump. Children with sensory issues may react with much more than just a startled response. They may protectively strike out, scream, even run away.

Avoid touching the child's hair, face, neck, and abdomen. These are the areas that are typically the most sensitive for children with tactile difficulties. However, in situations where health, hygiene, or safety are of concern, touching these areas may be unavoidable.

Use a firm rather than light touch. For many children, light touch creates an uncomfortable sensation, like a bug crawling on the skin. Few children with sensory integration problems find such a sensation tolerable.

Establish predictable, consistent routines. Children with sensory disorders must spend much mental energy modulating and processing the sensory information they take in from their surroundings. When the classroom environment is familiar, it leaves the children with fewer things to process and allows them to concentrate on tasks.

Supporting with materials

An important way to address the special needs of children with sensory processing difficulties is through the materials offered to them. Offering a variety and range of materials demonstrates developmentally appropriate practice for all children. For children with special needs, especially sensory integration needs, it encourages their continued participation in play activities (Brown 2006; Prestia 2004). Because the range of materials these children can or will use is more limited than for typically developing children, having a larger selection increases the odds they will find a choice that suits their comfort level. Teachers can offer, for example:

A variety of materials. For art media, for example, when children can choose between wooden sticks or cotton balls, or between crayons or finger paint, a wide variety of sensory sensibilities can be met. For writing tools, this might mean supplying grippers on pens and pencils, pencils with lead of varying hardness, ballpoint pens, mechanical pencils, markers, and paper of different thicknesses and textures. In the dramatic play area, children might have available items of varying textures, such as a rubber raincoat, chenille robe, silk gowns, corduroy jacket, ultrasuede throw blankets, and heavy work boots. The teacher might provide both hard, molded hand puppets and soft, plush hand puppets.

A variety of seating choices. The classroom should offer hard seating as well as soft; upright as well as slouchy. Children might be able to choose among bare chairs, chairs with cushions or foam wedges, firm floor pillows, squishy beanbags, and the floor. Children with tactile problems often prefer hammock or beanbag chairs that hug their bodies, providing more sensory stimulation (Brown 2006). Large rubber therapy balls can also be useful; the balls may help some children relax, while others may use them for balancing activities or for bouncing (Prestia 2004).

Other materials, although they can be enjoyed by any child, are particularly valuable for children with certain sensory difficulties. For example, teachers can provide:

Blocks covered with different textures, such as aluminum foil, sandpaper, or fabric—in addition to regular blocks—for tactilely hyposensitive children. A variety of textures allows them to feel the boundaries of blocks in ways the regular surfaces do not allow.

Exercise bands for preschool and elementary children with proprioceptive problems. The bands, which can be purchased at many general merchandise and sporting goods stores, can supply these children with the sensory input of resistance. Toddlers can push carts filled with heavy objects, such as phone books, to accomplish the same deep muscle pressure.

Supporting with activities

There are a variety of experiences to help children with sensory integration disorders learn to process physical sensation more appropriately. Teachers can engage toddlers and preschoolers in clapping games and can encourage dancing and swinging. Infants can be swung gently while being held or in a blanket swing (a blanket held at the corners by two adults).

Also useful for older toddlers and preschoolers are activities with balls, such as bouncing and catching, dribbling, or passing a ball from one child to another hand to hand. For infants, being rocked in a chair or bounced gently on the caregiver's knee or foot is a helpful activity. The teacher can also provide infants with floor toys to pick up and pass from hand to hand.

Regular exercises for toddlers and older children, such as push-ups, jumping jacks, hugging oneself, knee bends, and slow stretches, help build muscle strength and coordination, along with increasing their body awareness. Games of tug-of-war or obstacle courses that require crawling under large floor cushions are beneficial, as are opportunities to push or carry something heavy such as a phone book. Infants can have their arms and legs exercised during floor time or while on the changing table.

Meeting the needs of all children

When we talk about teaching diverse groups of children and providing the highest quality of services for them, we must take as a starting point our own beliefs about children and families. The mandate of inclusion requires teachers to become responsive to the special needs and abilities of *all* children as individuals. (Holliday, Parker, & Klein 1998: 99)

As always, activities for children with special needs should be developed in concert with trained professionals, such as occupational therapists. Different children will tolerate and thrive with different kinds of touch. As early childhood educators, we must work with families, therapists, and other professionals to tailor our practices to best suit all the children in our care.

References

Adams, C., & J. Fay. 1981. *No more secrets*. San Luis Obispo, CA: Impact.

Ahn, H.N., & N. Gilbert. 1992, September. Cultural diversity and sexual abuse prevention. *Social Service Review*, 410–27.

Ainsworth, M., M. Blehar, E. Waters, & S. Wall. 1978. *Patterns of attachment*. Hillsdale, NJ: Erlbaum.

Albus, K., & M. Dozier. 1999. Indiscriminate friendliness and terror of strangers in infancy: Contributions from the study of infants in foster care. *Infant Mental Health Journal* 20: 30–41.

Alderman, L. 2001. Hands-on therapy. *Chicopee* 81: H8.

American Academy of Pediatrics. 2000. Sexual abuse prevention. Located on the World Wide Web at www.medem.com/MedLB/article_detaillb.cfm?article_ID=ZZZ7PP1YA7C&sub_cat=355. Retrieved June 19, 2006.

Anderson, C. 2000, October/November. The touch continuum: Part of a risk-reduction curriculum. *SIECUS Report* 29 (1): 24–27. Available online at www.siecus.org/siecusreport/volume29/29-1.pdf.

Anderson, G., E. Moore, J. Hepworth, & N. Bergman. 2003. Early skin-to-skin contact for mothers and their healthy newborn infants. *The Cochrane Library* 2: 206–7.

Anisfeld, E., V. Casper, M. Nozyce, & M. Cunningham. 1990. Does infant carrying promote attachment? An experimental study of the effects of increased physical contact on the development of attachment. *Child Development* 61: 1617–27.

Appleton, J. 2005, 9 February. Losing touch. *Guardian*. Located on the World Wide Web at http://education.guardian.co.uk/schools/comment/story/0,,1409004,00.html. Retrieved March 4, 2006.

Aronson, S. 2002. *Healthy young children: A manual for programs*. 4th ed. Washington, DC: NAEYC.

Ayres, A.J. 2005. *Sensory integration and the child: Understanding hidden sensory challenges*. 25th anniv. ed. Los Angeles: Western Psychological Services.

Baker, A., & L. Manfredi/Petitt. 2004. *Relationships, the heart of quality care: Creating community among adults in early care settings*. Washington, DC: NAEYC.

Bar-Haim, Y., B. Sutton, N. Fox, & R. Marvin. 2000. Stability and change of attachment at 14, 24, and 58 months of age: Behavior, representation, and life events. *Journal of Child Psychology and Psychiatry and Allied Disciplines* 41: 381–88.

Barker, S. 2005. *The cuddle factor*. Located on the World Wide Web at www.oxytocin.org. Retrieved on November 10, 2005.

Berggren, S. 2004, September. Massage in schools reduces stress and anxiety. *Young Children* 59 (5): 67–68.

Berk, L.E. 2006. Looking at kindergarten children. In *K today: Teaching and learning in the kindergarten year*, ed. D.F. Gullo, 11–25. Washington, DC: NAEYC.

Blackwell, P.L. 2000. The influence of touch on child development: Implications for intervention. *Infants & Young Children* 13: 25–39.

Bolen, R. 2003. Child sexual abuse: Prevention or promotion? *Social Work* 48 (2): 174–85.

Bos, B. 1978. *Don't move the muffin tins: A hands-off guide to art for the young child.* Roseville, CA: Turn-the-Page Press.

Bower, B. 2000, May 27. Attachment disorder draws closer look. *Science News* 157 (22): 343–46.

Bowlby, J. [1969] 2000. *Attachment and loss.* New York: Basic Books.

Bowlby, J. 1980. *Attachment and loss. Vol. 3: Attachment.* New York: Basic Books.

Boyd, D., & H. Bee. 2006. *Lifespan development.* Boston: Pearson Education.

Bredekamp, S., & C. Copple, eds. 1997. *Developmentally appropriate practice in early childhood programs.* Rev. ed. Washington, DC: NAEYC.

Briere, J., & D.M. Elliot. 2003. Prevalence and psychological sequence of self-reported childhood physical and sexual abuse in a general population sample of men and women. *Child Abuse and Neglect* 27: 10.

Broadhurst, D., M. Edmunds, & R. MacDicken. 1979. *Early childhood programs and prevention treatment of child abuse and neglect.* User Manual Series. Washington, DC: U.S. Department of Health, Education, and Welfare.

Brown, J. 2006, February 9. Innovative chair provides calming hug; may help youths who have sensory motor problems. *The Boston Globe*, 5.

Cantu, C.C. 2002. An introduction to early childhood sensory integration. *The Exceptional Parent* 32 (4): 47–55.

Carlson, F.M. 2003. Incorporating touch to prevent child sexual abuse. *National Child Advocate* 5 (2): 5–9.

Casper, R. 1999. Characteristics of children who experience positive or negative reactions to a sexual abuse prevention program. *Journal of Child Sexual Abuse* 7 (4): 97–112.

Child & Family Canada. 2000. Child sexual abuse prevention initiatives. Located on the World Wide Web at www.cfc-efc.ca/docs/vocfc/00000069.htm. Retrieved on June 19, 2006.

Chisholm, K. 1998. A three year follow-up of attachment and indiscriminate friendliness in children adopted from Romanian orphanages. *Child Development* 69: 1092–106.

Chrisman, K., & D. Couchenour. 2002. *Healthy sexuality development: A guide for early childhood educators and families.* Washington, DC: NAEYC.

Chrisman, K., & D. Couchenour. 2004, March/April. Healthy sexuality development in young children. *Child Care Information Exchange,* 34–36.

Cigales, M., T. Field, Z. Hossain, M. Pelaz-Nogueras, & T. Gerwitz. 1996. Touch among children at nursery school. *Early Child Development & Care* 126: 101–10.

Cohn, J., & E.Z. Tronick. 1989. Specificity of infants' response to mothers' affective behavior. *Journal of the American Academy of Child and Adolescent Psychiatry* 28 (2): 242–48.

Copple, C., & S. Bredekamp. 2006. *Basics of developmentally appropriate practice: An introduction for teachers of children 3 to 6.* Washington, DC: NAEYC.

Council for Professional Recognition. 1999. *CDA assessment observation instrument.* Washington, DC: Author.

Cullen, L., & J. Barlow. 2002. Parents' experiences of caring for children with autism and attending a touch therapy programme. *Child Care in Practice* 8 (1): 35–45.

Davis, K., & C. Gidyez. 2000. Child sexual abuse prevention programs: A meta-analysis. *Journal of Clinical Child Psychology* 29 (2): 257–65.

Del Prete, T. 1997. Hands off? The touchy subject of touching. *The Education Digest* 62 (7): 59–61.

Del Prete, T. 1998. Getting back in touch with students: Should we risk it? *Professional School Counseling* 1 (4): 62–65.

Dodge, D.T., & T.S. Bickart. 1998. *Preschool for parents: What every parent needs to know about preschool.* Washington, DC: Teaching Strategies.

Elliott, M. 1995. Child sexual abuse prevention: What offenders tell us. *Child Abuse & Neglect* 19 (5): 579–94.

Escalona, A., T. Field, R. Singer-Strunck, C. Cullen, & K. Hartshorn. 2001. Brief report: Improvements in the behavior of children with autism following massage therapy. *Journal of Autism and Developmental Disorders* 31 (5): 513–16.

Faller, K.C. 1993. *Child sexual abuse: Intervention and treatment issues.* Washington, DC: U.S. Department of Health and Human Services, Administration for Children and Families, National Center on Child Abuse and Neglect. Available online at www.childwelfare.gov/pubs/usermanuals/sexabuse/sexabuse.pdf.

Farquhar, S.E. 2001. Moral panic in New Zealand: Teachers touching children. In *Touchy subject: Teachers touching children,* ed. A. Jones, 87–98. New Zealand: University of Otago Press.

Farquhar, S.E. 2005. *How to pick remarkable quality childcare and education.* New Zealand: Childforum Research Network.

Ferber, S., & I. Makhoul. 2004. The effect of skin-to-skin contact (kangaroo care) shortly after birth on the neurobehavioral responses of the term newborn: A randomized, controlled trial. *Pediatrics* 113 (4): 858–65. Available online at www.pediatrics.org.

Field, T. ed. 1999. *Touch in early development.* Hillsdale, NJ: Erlbaum.

Field, T. 2001. *Touch.* Cambridge, MA: MIT Press.

Field, T. 2002. Violence and touch deprivation in adolescents. *Adolescence* 37 (148): 735–49.

Field, T., J. Harding, B. Soliday, D. Lasko, N. Gonzalez, & C. Valdeon. 1994. Touching in infant, toddler, and preschool nurseries. *Early Child Development and Care* 98: 115–20.

Field, T., M. Hernandez-Reif, M. Diego, L. Feijo, Y. Vera, & K. Gil. 2004. Massage therapy by parents improves early growth and development. *Infant Behavior & Development* 27 (4): 435–42.

Field, T., M. Hernandez-Reif, M. Diego, S. Schanberg, & C. Kuhn. 2005. Cortisol decreases and serotonin and dopamine increase following massage therapy. *International Journal of Neuroscience* 115 (10): 1397–413.

Field, T., M. Hernandez-Reif, S. Hart, O. Quintino, L. Drose, T. Field, C. Kuhn, & S. Schanberg. 1997a. Effects of sexual abuse are lessened by massage therapy. *Journal of Bodywork and Movement Therapies* 1 (2): 65–69.

Field, T., D. Lasko, P. Mundy, T. Henteleff, S. Kabat, S. Talpins, & M. Dowling. 1997b. Brief report: Autistic children's attentiveness and responsivity improve after touch therapy. *Journal of Autism and Developmental Disorders* 27 (3): 333–38.

Field, T., S. Schanberg, & F. Scafidi. 1986. Tactile/kinesthetic stimulation effects on preterm neonates. *Pediatrician* 77: 654–58.

Furman, L., & J. Kennell. 2000. Breastmilk and skin-to-skin kangaroo care for premature infants. Avoiding bonding failure. *Acta Paediatrica* 89: 1280–83.

Gartrell, D. 2004. *The power of guidance: Teaching social-emotional skills in early childhood classrooms.* Clifton Park, NY: Thomson/Delmar Learning; Washington, DC: NAEYC.

Gilbert, N. 1994, March. Touch and stop. *Reason* 10: 52–53.

Gould, P., & J. Sullivan. 1999. *The inclusive early childhood classroom: Easy ways to adapt learning centers for all children.* Beltsville, MD: Gryphon House.

Greenman, J., & A. Stonehouse. 1996. *Prime times.* St. Paul, MN: Redleaf Press.

Greenspan, S. 2004. Working with the child who has sensory integration disorder. *Early Childhood Today* 18 (7): 20–22.

Harris, C. 1999, July/August. The mystery of ticklish laughter. *American Scientist* 87: 344–51.

Harrison-Speake, K., & F. Willis. 1995. Ratings of the appropriateness of touch among family members. *Journal of Nonverbal Behavior* 19 (2): 85–100.

Hart, B., & T. Risley. 1995. *Meaningful differences in the everyday experience of young American children.* Baltimore: Brookes.

Hart, C. 1996. *Secrets of serotonin.* New York: Lynn Sonberg Book Associates.

Hart-Rossi, J. 1984. *Protect your child from sexual abuse: A parent's guide.* Seattle, WA: Parenting Press. [Personal Bubble exercise adapted from Adams & Fay 1981]

Hatch-Rasmussen, C. 1995. Sensory integration. Located on the World Wide Web at www.autism.org/si.html. Retrieved on June 29, 2006.

Hernandez-Reif, M., T. Field, S. Largie, M. Diego, N. Manigat, J. Seoanes, & J. Bornstein. 2005. Cerebral palsy symptoms in children decreased following massage therapy. *Early Child Development & Care* 175 (5): 445–56.

Hewlett, B.S. 1996. Diverse contexts of human infancy. In *Cross-cultural research for social science*, eds. C. Ember & M. Ember, 287–97. Englewood Cliffs, NJ: Prentice Hall.

Hockenberry, M., D. Wilson, & M. Winkelstein. 2005. *Wong's essentials of pediatric nursing*. St. Louis, MO: Elsevier Mosby.

Holden, C. 1996. Small refugees suffer the effects of early neglect. *Science* 274: 1076–77.

Holliday, S., & D.M. Parker, with S.M. Klein. 1998. Including everyone. In *When teachers reflect: Journeys toward effective, inclusive practice*, eds. E.A. Tertell, S.M. Klein, & J.L. Jewett, 99–118. Washington, DC: NAEYC.

Honig, A.S. 1998, August. Attachment and relationships: Beyond parenting. Paper presented at the Head Start Quality Network Research Satellite Conference, East Lansing, MI.

Honig, A.S. 2000, March/April. Sexuality and young children. *Child Care Information Exchange*, 27–29.

Honig, A.S. 2002. *Secure relationships: Nurturing infant-toddler attachment in early care settings*. Washington, DC: NAEYC.

Honig, A.S. 2004, September. Read your baby's body language. *Scholastic Parent & Child*, 25–26.

Hunter, J.A., A.J. Figueredo, N.M. Malamuth, & J.V. Becker. 2003. Juvenile sex offenders: Toward the development of a typology. *Sexual Abuse: A Journal of Research and Treatment* 15 (1): 27–48.

Johnson & Johnson, Inc. 1995. *Touch in labor and infancy: Clinical implications*. Located on the World Wide Web at www.khjpaed.org/johnson/TouchinLabourAndInfancy/index.htm. Retrieved on June 30, 2006.

Jones, A., & A. Yarbrough. 1985. A naturalistic study of the meanings of touch. *Communication Monographs* 52: 19–56.

Kaminski, M., T. Pellino, & J. Wish. 2002. Play and pets: The physical and emotional impact of child-life and pet therapy on hospitalized children. *Children's Health Care* 31 (4): 321–35.

Kaufman, K., J. Holmberg, K. Orts, & F. McCrady. 1998. Factors influencing sexual offenders' modus operandi: An examination of victim offender relatedness and age. *Child Maltreatment* 3: 349–61.

Kraizer, S., S. Witte, & G. Fryer, Jr. 1989, Sept.-Oct. Child sexual abuse prevention programs: What makes them effective in protecting children? *Children Today* 18 (5): 23–27. Available online at http://www.findarticles.com/p/articles/mi_m1053/is_n5_v18/ai_8153035.

Kranowitz, C.S. 2005. *The out-of-sync child: Recognizing and coping with sensory processing disorder*. New York: Penguin.

Kranowitz, C.S. 2006. *The out-of-sync child: Recognizing and coping with sensory processing disorder*. Rev. ed. New York: Penguin.

Lally, J.R., & K. Oldershaw. 2005. *Brain development*. The Program for Infant/Toddler Caregivers. [Unpublished handout from training session, Module III, Brain Development in Infancy and How to Facilitate It]. Located on the World Wide Web at www.pitc.org/cs/pitclib/view/pitc_res/118. Retrieved on November 7, 2005.

Lanning, B., D. Ballard, & J. Robinson III. 1999. Child sexual abuse prevention programs in Texas public elementary schools. *The Journal of School Health* 69 (1): 3–8.

Lawson, M.B. 1998. Physical contact between teachers and preschool-age children in early childhood programs. Doctoral dissertation, University of Massachusetts, Amherst, Massachusetts.

Levy, T.M., & M. Orlans. 1998. *Attachment, trauma, and healing: Understanding and treating attachment disorder in children and families*. Washington, DC: CWLA Press.

Major, B., A. Schmidlin, & L. Williams. 1990. Gender patterns in social touch: The impact of setting and age. *Journal of Personality and Social Psychology* 58: 634–43.

Marcellus, L., ed. 2000. *Safe babies: A caregivers guide to daily care for infants exposed prenatally to alcohol and drugs*. Vancouver, BC: Ministry of Children and Family Development.

Marotz, L., M. Cross, & J. Rush. 2005. *Health, safety, and nutrition for the young child.* 6th ed. Clifton Park, NY: Thomson/Delmar Learning.

Mazur, S., & C. Pekor. 1985. Can teachers touch children anymore? Physical contact and its values in child development. *Young Children* 40 (4): 10–12.

Mill, D., & D. Romano-White. 1999. Correlates of affectionate and angry behavior in child care educators of preschool-aged children. *Early Childhood Research Quarterly* 14: 155–78.

Mitchell-Copeland, J., S. Denham, & E.K. DeMulder. 1997. Q-sort assessment of child-teacher attachment relationships and social competence in preschool. *Early Education and Development* 8: 27–39.

Moberg, K. 2003. *The oxytocin factor.* Cambridge, MA: Da Capo Press.

Montagu, A. 1986. *Touching: The human significance of the skin.* 3d ed. New York: Harper & Row.

Morrow, C., T. Field, & F. Scafidi. 1991. Differential effects of massage and heelstick procedures on transcutaneous oxygen tension in preterm neonates. *Infant Behavior and Development* 14: 397–414.

Nackley, V. 2006. Sensory diet applications and environmental modifications: A winning combination. Henry Occupational Therapy Services, Inc. Located on the World Wide Web at http://henryot.com/news/sensory_diet_applications_review.asp. Retrieved on April 21, 2006.

NAEYC. 1996. Prevention of child abuse in early childhood programs and the responsibilities of early childhood professionals to prevent child abuse. Position Statement. Washington, DC: Author. Available online at www.naeyc.org/about/positions/pdf/pschab98.pdf.

NAEYC. 1997 [adopted July 1996]. Developmentally appropriate practice in early childhood programs serving children from birth through age 8. Position Statement. In *Developmentally appropriate practice in early childhood programs*, rev. ed., eds. S. Bredekamp & C. Copple, 3–30. Washington, DC: Author. Available online at www.naeyc.org/about/positions/pdf/PSDAP98.PDF.

NAEYC. 2005a, April. NAEYC code of ethical conduct and statement of commitment. Position Statement. Washington, DC: Author. Available online at www.naeyc.org/about/positions/pdf/PSETH05.PDF.

NAEYC. 2005b. *NAEYC early childhood program standards and accreditation criteria: The mark of quality in early childhood education.* Washington, DC: Author. Text of the standards and criteria available online at www.naeyc.org/accreditation/standardscriteria/.

Neill, S. 1991. Children's responses to touch. *British Educational Research Journal* 17 (2): 149–63.

Nelson, B.G. 2002. *The importance of men teachers and reasons why there are so few: A survey of members of NAEYC.* Minneapolis, MN: MenTeach.

Nelson, B.G. 2004, November/December. Myths about men who work with young children. *Child Care Information Exchange* 160: 16–18.

Neuman, S., C. Copple, & S. Bredekamp. 2000. *Learning to read and write: Developmentally appropriate practices for young children.* Washington, DC: NAEYC.

Noddings, N. [1984] 2003. *Caring: A feminine approach to ethics and moral education.* 2d ed. Berkeley, CA: University of Berkeley Press.

Oesterreich, L., & K. Shirer. 1994. *Sexual abuse of children: Understanding abuse.* National Network for Child Care. Located on the World Wide Web at www.nncc.org/Abuse/sex.abuse.html. Retrieved on February 5, 2001.

Pellegrini, A.D., & P.K. Smith. 1994. Physical activity play: The nature and function of a neglected aspect of play. *Child Development* 69 (3): 577–98.

Perdue, V., & J. Connor. 1978. Patterns of touching between preschool children and male and female teachers. *Child Development* 49: 1258–62.

Piaget, J. 1952. *The origins of intelligence in children.* New York: International Universities Press.

Pinon, M., T. Hulsey, & A. Woodland. 1999. Improving preschoolers' comprehension of sex abuse prevention concepts through video repetition. *Journal of Child Sexual Abuse* 8 (2): 77–92.

Piper, H., & H. Smith. 2003. Touch in educational and child care settings: Dilemmas & responses. *British Educational Research Journal* 29 (6): 879–93.

Pirtle, S. 1998. *Linking up! Using music, movement, and language arts to promote caring, cooperation, and communication.* Cambridge, MA: Educators for Social Responsibility.

Plummer, C.A. [1993] 2005. Child sexual abuse prevention is appropriate and successful. In *Current controversies in family violence*, 2d ed., eds. D. Loseke, R. Gelles, & M. Cavanaugh, 257–70. Thousand Oaks, CA: Sage.

Prairie, A.P. 2005. *Inquiry into math, science, and technology for teaching young children.* Clifton Park, NY: Thomson Delmar Learning.

Prescott, J. 1975, November. Body pleasure and the origins of violence. *Bulletin of the Atomic Scientists*, 11–20.

Prestia, K. 2004. Incorporate sensory activities and choices into the classroom. *Intervention in School and Clinic* 39 (3): 172–75.

Putnam, F. 2003. Child sexual abuse. *Journal of the American Academy of Child and Adolescent Psychiatry* 42 (3): 269–78.

Reilly, J., & S. Martin. 1995. Protecting the children as we protect ourselves. *Child Care Center Connection* 4 (6). Located on the World Wide Web at www.nncc.org/Abuse/cc46_protect.child.html. Retrieved on February 5, 2001.

Rice, C., & D. Goessling. 2005. Recruiting and retaining male special education teachers. *Remedial and Special Education* 26 (6): 347–56.

Richardson, H. 1997, Winter. Kangaroo care: Why does it work? *Midwifery Today*, 50–51. Available online at www.midwiferytoday.com/articles/kangaroocare.asp.

Rothbaum, F., A. Grauer, & D. Rubin. 1997. Becoming sexual: Differences between child and adult sexuality. *Young Children* 52 (6): 22–28.

Scafidi, F., T. Field, & S. Schanberg. 1990. Massage stimulates growth in preterm infants: A replication. *Infant Behavior and Development* 13: 167–88.

Schaaf, R., & L. Miller. 2005. Occupational therapy using a sensory integrative approach for children with developmental disabilities. *Mental Retardation and Developmental Disabilities Research Reviews* 11: 143–48.

Scott, E., & J. Panksepp. 2003. Rough-and-tumble play in human children. *Aggressive Behavior* 29: 539–51.

Shakeshaft, C. 2004. *Educator sexual misconduct: A synthesis of existing literature.* Washington, DC: U.S. Department of Education.

Shakeshaft, C., & A. Cohan. 1995. Sexual abuse of students by school personnel. *Phi Delta Kappan* 76 (7): 512–20.

Shore, R. 1997. *Rethinking the brain: New insights into early development.* New York: Families and Work Institute.

SIECUS Early Childhood Task Force. 1998. *Right from the start: Guidelines for sexuality issues birth to five years.* New York: SIECUS.

Small, M. 1998. *Our babies, ourselves.* New York: Anchor.

Smith, P.K. 1995. Play, ethology, and education: A personal account. In *The future of play theory*, ed. A. Pellegrini, 3–21. Albany, NY: State University of New York Press.

South Carolina Educational Television. 1984. Seeing infants with new eyes [video]. Produced by SCETV.

Spungen, C., S. Jensen, & N. Finkelstein. 1989. Child personal safety: Model program for prevention of child sexual abuse. *Social Work* 34 (2): 127–31.

Strickland, J., & S. Reynolds. 1988, December. The new untouchables: Risk management of child abuse in child care—Policies and procedures. *Child Care Information Exchange*, 33–36.

Tabachnick, J. 2003. Create a social marketing campaign. *National Child Advocate* 5 (2): 1–10.

Telljohann, S., S. Everett, & J. Price. 1997. Evaluation of a third grade sexual abuse curriculum. *The Journal of School Health* 67 (4): 149–53.

Tobin, J. 1997. *Making a place for pleasure in early childhood education.* New Haven, CT: Yale University Press.

Trelease, J. 2001. *The read-aloud handbook.* 5th ed. New York: Penguin Books.

Tutty, L. 2000. What children learn from sexual abuse prevention programs: Difficult concepts and developmental issues. *Research on Social Work Practice* 10 (3): 275–300.

Twardosz, S., & V.M. Nordquist. 1983. The development and importance of affection. In *Advances in clinical psychology,* eds. B.B. Lahey and A.E. Kazden, 129–68. New York: Plenum Press.

U.S. Department of Health and Human Services, Administration on Children, Youth and Families. 2006. *Child maltreatment 2004.* Washington, DC: U.S. Government Printing Office. Available online at www.acf.dhhs.gov/programs/cb/pubs/cm04/index.htm.

U.S. Government Accountability Office. 2005. *Report to the chairman and ranking minority member, Subcommittee on Human Rights and Wellness, Committee on Government Reform, U.S. House of Representatives. Special education: Children with autism.* Washington, DC: Author.

Waters, E., & E.M. Cummings. 2000, February. A secure base from which to explore close relationships. *Child Development* 71: 164–72.

Weisberg, P. 1975. Developmental differences in children's preferences for high- and low-arousing forms of contact stimulation. *Child Development* 46: 975–79.

Weller, A., & R. Feldman. 2003. Emotion regulation and touch in infants: The role of cholecystokinin and opioids. *Peptides* 24 (5): 779–88.

Wilkerson, J. 1994. Training families to teach their children about sexual abuse prevention: Parent and child outcomes. Doctoral dissertation, University of Cincinnati, Cincinnati, Ohio.

Willmarth, C. 2001. Read with me: Reading aloud with children in early childhood settings. Capstone project, Concordia University, Saint Paul, Minnesota.

Yeargin-Allsopp, M., C. Rice, T. Karapurkar, N. Doernberg, C. Boyle, & C. Murphy. 2003. Prevalence of autism in a U.S. metropolitan area. *The Journal of the American Medical Association* 289 (1): 49–55.

Resources

For further reading

In addition to the useful resources below, see the **References** list for many others.

Idaho Department of Health and Welfare. *Infant massage.* Located on the World Wide Web at http://healthandwelfare.idaho.gov/DesktopModules/ArticlesSortable/ArticlesSrtView.aspx? tabID=0&ItemID=663&mid=10429. Retrieved June 5, 2006.

Johnson, R.T. 2000. *Hands-off!: The disappearance of touch in the care of children.* New York: Peter Lang.

Keating, K. 1995. *Hug therapy.* New York: MJF Books.

McClure, V. 2000. *Infant massage: A handbook for loving parents.* New York: Bantam Books.

Powell, A. 1998, April 9. Children need touching and attention, Harvard researchers say. *Harvard University Gazette.* Located on the World Wide Web at www.news.harvard.edu/gazette/1998/04.09/ChildrenNeedTou.html. Retrieved July 10, 2006.

Books for children about touch

In addition to titles about touch such as those below, there are many books that feature fabric or other materials for children to touch and feel, such as *Pat the Bunny* (by D. Kunhardt).

A very touching book . . . for little people and for big people, rev. ed., by J. Hindman

Because it's my body! , by J. Sherman

Bodies, by B. Brenner

Daddy hugs, by M. Cocca-Leffler

Hug, by J. Alborough

It's MY body. L. Freeman

Loving touches, by L. Freeman

The giant hug, by S. Horning

Web sites

Child Welfare Information Gateway—www.childwelfare.gov

Provides information and resources to help protect children and strengthen families. Specifically addresses child abuse and neglect, supporting families, and out-of-home care.

The Gentle Touch Parent-Child Program—www.gentletouchparent-child.com

Details a parenting program that emphasizes massage, communication, and nurturing. Also includes links for parents and professionals, including many medical links.

National Association for the Education of Young Children—www.naeyc.org

Features position statements, accreditation standards and criteria, and many useful resources for teachers and teacher educators, including NAEYC's books, journal and online journal.

The Natural Child Project: Resources for Caring Parents—www.naturalchild.org

Geared specifically toward parents, this site includes many links for research articles, books, and other Web sites, all of which focus on helping parents make decisions that contribute to a loving, supportive environment for children.

Touch Research Institute (TRI)—www.miami.edu/touch-research

Learn about TRI's work concerning the study of touch and its application in science and medicine. Also browse information regarding the institute's research, newsletter, workshops, and books.

Zero to Three—www.zerotothree.org

Provides resources, including a professional journal and a variety of books, for educators and parents that focus on the first three years of life. Also includes a helpful, well-organized section detailing public policy.

Appendixes

This Appendix section contains resources to support efforts to include positive, nurturing touch in young children's lives by implementing a healthy and appropriate touch component in early education programs. No permission is needed to reproduce and adapt this material for a program's individual needs.

Information on detecting and reporting child sexual abuse is provided in **Appendix A.** Sample policy language on appropriate touch that can be adapted for both staff and family handbooks is provided in **Appendix B.**

Note that the material offered here addresses necessary guidance components in only a general way. For some elements, such as mandated reporting or criminal record checks, the governing legislation will vary from state to state. Administrators must do their homework when developing specific policies for their individual school, center, agency, or organization. Legal review also is recommended to ensure that policies comply with all applicable federal, state, city, and local laws and regulations.

Sample family letters and a family questionnaire related to issues of touch in early childhood settings are provided in **Appendix C.**

Appendix D offers outlines for training sessions, because providing training to teachers makes those teachers more likely to exhibit more affectionate physical behavior toward children (Mill & Romano-White 1999). Each outline begins by listing the learning goal for the session. During the actual session, it is important that participants have the opportunity to state their own learning goals, too, and to relate the information being presented to their own lives and experiences. To help accomplish these objectives, sample reflection questions and key points to cover also are listed.

Families also can benefit from training. Like staff members, families are better equipped to follow and support policies that they understand. Training can help emphasize for families the importance of touch in the early years and highlight the ways in which a program can offer touch while safeguarding children. The family letters in **Appendix C** can be used to both alert families to upcoming trainings and inform them about the topic before the training.

Detecting and Reporting Child Sexual Abuse

Employees of early childhood programs are mandated to report suspected child abuse of any kind. Being a mandated reporter means you are under a legal obligation to make a report of any suspicion of child abuse, whether physical, emotional, sexual, or neglect. Training should be provided annually in recognizing all types of abuse, reporting suspicion of child abuse, and preventing abuse. Staff and parents who would like more clarification on this issue should feel free to talk to program or school administrators.

Detecting suspected abuse

When a child has been victimized by abusive touch, often there are signs and symptoms. These signs are both physical and behavioral, and vary according to the age of the child (Broadhurst, Edmunds, & MacDicken 1979; Faller 1993). Physical signs that sexual abuse *might* have occurred are that the child has:

- torn, stained, or bloody underclothes,
- pain or itching in the genital area,
- difficulty walking or sitting,
- genital or anal injury,
- presence of a sexually transmitted disease, or

• frequent urinary or yeast infections not attributable to poor hygiene, bubble baths, or antibiotics.

Emotional or behavioral signs that sexual abuse *might* have occurred are that the child:

• is withdrawn or chronically depressed,

• demonstrates having sexual knowledge not ordinarily possessed by young children (e.g., sexually explicit comments in conversation, drawings of sexual acts, sexual aggression toward younger children, sexual gestures to adults, sexual interactions with dolls or stuffed animals, or attempted sexual activity with peers),

• is overly concerned for siblings,

• has problems or resists involvement with peers,

• experiences sudden significant weight change (loss or gain),

• exhibits hysteria or lack of emotional control,

• suddenly has difficulties in school, or

• feels threatened by physical contact or closeness.

Reporting suspected abuse

All 50 states have passed some form of mandatory child abuse and neglect reporting legislation in order to qualify for funding under the federal Child Abuse Prevention and Treatment Act (CAPTA). The Act defines *child abuse or neglect* as

> At a minimum, any recent act or failure to act on the part of a parent or caretaker, which results in death, serious physical or emotional harm, sexual abuse or exploitation, or an act or failure to act which presents an imminent risk of serious harm.

Further, the Act defines *sexual abuse* as

> The employment, use, persuasion, inducement, enticement, or coercion of any child to engage in, or assist any other person to engage in, any sexually explicit conduct or simulation of such conduct; ... or the rape, and in cases of caretaker or interfamilial relationships, statutory rape, molestation, prostitution, or other form of sexual exploitation of children, or incest with children. (Title 42 *U.S. Code*, Chapt. 67)

All states require certain professionals, including child care providers, teachers, and other school personnel, as well as institutions to report suspected child abuse.

For specific information about reporting statutes and child abuse prevention laws in your state, see the federal Child Welfare Information Gateway Web site, located online at www. childwelfare.gov/. There you can view all or selected child protection laws by state or in side-by-side compilations at www.childwelfare.gov/systemwide/laws_policies/search/.

In every state, reports must be made to some type of law enforcement authority or child protection agency when child abuse is suspected. Reporting to a parent or relative does not satisfy this legal duty under the statutes. A teacher or caregiver who feels uncomfortable making the report might prefer to give the information to the center director or to another designated administrator in the chain of command so that person can make the report instead. However, a state's individual law determines whether the suspicious teacher must make the report directly or whether the mandate to report is fulfilled by such a chain-of-command report to a third party.

When preparing employee or parent guidebooks, program staff would be wise to include the specifics of their state's requirements: "The mandated reporting requirement in our state is . . . " and "Failure to report suspected child abuse can result in criminal liability; in our state, the penalty for failure to report is. . . ."

Every teacher should be aware, therefore, of whether the legal mandate to report is met by reporting to a third party instead of reporting directly to a local child and family service authority. Either way, ultimately the legal mandate to report to someone is the teacher's.

A list of reporting agency phone numbers by state is provided on the Child Welfare Information Gateway Web site. To make a report of suspected child sexual abuse typically requires the following information (Marotz, Cross, & Rush 2005):

• The name and address of the child.

• Parent/guardian name and address.

• Action (if any) taken by the reporting individual.

• The child's age.

• The nature and extent of the child's injuries, including any evidence of previous injuries.

• The identity of the offending adult.

• Other information that could be helpful in establishing the cause of the child's injuries.

• The name, address, telephone number, and professional title of the individual making the report.

• Anecdotal notes recording accurate observations of the child's physical and emotional state over several days or weeks.

Sample Handbook Policies on Appropriate Touch

Incorporating appropriate touch in the classroom

Here at *[name of school or program]*, we believe in the importance of positive touch for the healthy development of young children. Touch reduces stress, aids healthy brain and emotional development, and demonstrates love for the children in our care. Appropriate touch in early education settings can be defined as nonintrusive, causing no feelings of discomfort or confusion for children. Such contact should also not cause feelings of discomfort or confusion to caregivers. Each child should be allowed to determine what kinds of touches he or she finds acceptable. With support from families, teachers can help inform children's understanding with appropriate guidance and instruction. Training on teaching children about appropriate touch is offered to our teachers at the time of employment and periodically thereafter.

So they use touch appropriately with children, staff are asked to follow these guidelines:

❐ Remember that physical contact is valuable to children. Let the child lead in showing you what kind of touch is acceptable to him or her.

❐ In general, avoid using touch with children if you are the only supervising adult. If possible, have another adult or some type of surveillance present.

❐ Ask permission before touching children. For example, say to a child, "Can I give you a hug?" If the child says no, then refrain from hugging him or her.

❐ Try to touch nonvulnerable body parts only, such as the shoulders, back, arms, and hands. Likewise, avoid vulnerable body parts, such as the chest, hair, and genitals, if possible.

❐ Be aware of cultural considerations when touching children. What is acceptable in some cultures is prohibited in others. Again, let the child lead.

❐ Be aware of a child's activity level and do not interrupt the child's engaged play with touch.

❐ Understand that a child's need for physical contact varies individually. Get to know each child and determine what kind of touch is appropriate.

❐ If you must touch a child's vulnerable areas—such as during diapering—tell the child which parts you are touching and why. Use the proper names for body parts. For example, say "I am cleaning your penis with a wipe to make sure all the urine is washed off. Cleaning your skin keeps it healthy."

❐ As children begin the toilet learning process, encourage them to share responsibility for cleaning their own genitals. You can offer them a flushable wipe and instruct them on how to wipe themselves. You can then tell them you will check to see that they are clean. Again, if you need to touch vulnerable areas, name which parts you are touching and why.

❐ In general, when deciding whether a touch is or is not appropriate, use the Touch Test: Ask yourself whether the touch would be appropriate if given to a stranger. For example, a handshake would be appropriate with a stranger, but a kiss would be inappropriate with a stranger.

Using touch for restraint

Here at *[name of school or program]*, we advocate the use of nurturing touch for the optimum growth of our children. We also advocate for children's inherent right to accept and refuse touch as they see fit for their own personal comfort.

There are times, though, when a child's safety is at stake. When this happens, we may use touch without the child's permission. Examples would include to keep a child from harm (e.g., physically preventing a child from running into the street or from falling off of climbing equipment) and to stop a child from harming himself or herself or another person.

When touch is used for restraint, a teacher might hold the child to keep him or her safe; generally the teacher will hold her arms around the child, with the child's body facing *away* from the teacher. Teachers will use a calm, soothing voice to remind children that they are only being held long enough to ensure their safety and the safety of others. If physical restraint is used with a child, the parents or guardians will be notified immediately.

Children will never be bound or held down in a face-down position, as these actions are physically and emotionally harmful. Children will not be threatened with restrictive holding in an effort to control their behavior. Also, teachers are encouraged to reflect on what changes could be made either to the environment or to adult expectations of children's behavior that could possibly preclude the need for physical restraint.

Restraining touch will only be used under the supervision of another adult, preferably an adult in a position of responsibility (e.g., a school administrator or center director). If the need to physically restrain a child recurs persistently, a team of people that includes family members, teachers, administrators, and appropriate specialists will meet and work together to identify the problem and establish preventative strategies. Physical restraint is not a long-term solution. Instead, it is a short-term intervention that will be used only in extreme circumstances and with at least two supervising adults.

Hiring safeguards

Here at *[name of school or program]*, positions with our program are contingent on both a clear criminal record check and satisfactory professional references. To protect both the children in our care and our staff, the following policies are in place in our program:

Pre-employment criminal record check

This program has a policy on employing persons with criminal records in our facilities. Any person who has been convicted of committing a felony offense, of neglecting or abusing a dependent person, or of committing a sexual offense will not be allowed to work in our facility. Convictions for other offenses also may preclude employment.

Before being hired, potential employees are required to demonstrate a clear criminal record. Criminal record checks are good for a 12-month period and must be renewed yearly; employees may be terminated if at any time they fail to receive a clear criminal record check.

Before being hired, potential employees may also be subject to a state fingerprint record check or an FBI fingerprint record check or both. This fingerprint record check may be required by law. If such a check is necessary for employment in this program, potential employees will be notified of this at the same time that the criminal record check is obtained.

Pre-employment professional reference check

Verification of professional references (e.g., from supervisor, HR department) is an essential part of a responsible early education program. We require at least two positive professional references on an applicant before we will make a job offer. If the applicant does not have a history of employment, or if we cannot verify the history, we will consider personal references (e.g., from teachers, friends, coworkers) to fulfill this professional reference requirement.

The two references can be provided verbally or in writing. The applicant must give permission to contact the references, and must provide contact information.

Environmental features

[The following list is an example of the types of features a program may want to highlight in their staff or parent handbook. You will want to customize your text to match your program's facilities.]

Here at [name of school or program], we strive to offer a safe environment by providing safety features that help protect both the teachers and the children in our care. At our facility, we have:

❏ observation panels into each room

❏ at least two adults present in each room, when possible

❏ close-circuit cameras in each room

❏ "open-door" access to each room (e.g., families are encouraged to drop by unannounced; individual classrooms are not locked)

❏ windows between classrooms so teachers can observe and support each other

Appendix C

Sample Family Letters and Family Questionnaire

The importance of touch in young children's lives

Dear Family Members,

In our early childhood program, we value your child's physical, emotional, social, and cognitive development. Because we value your participation in our program and want you to be aware of how we care for your child, we are sending this letter about the ways we use positive and nurturing touch to support your child's growth.

We strive to incorporate positive touch into daily routines and activities as much as possible. We do this because research consistently demonstrates that touch is necessary for healthy brain and emotional development.

Our staff members have received training to ensure that the physical contact children experience in the classroom is appropriate and beneficial. We also provide a workshop for families to share what we know about the importance of touch with young children. We hope you'll attend this workshop the next time it is offered. For more information on our policies, please see our *Family Handbook* or talk to our Director.

In our program, we advocate for children's inherent right to accept and refuse touch as they see fit for their own personal comfort. There are times, though, when a child's safety may be compromised; when this happens, touch may be used without a child's permission. For example, a teacher might keep a child from harm by blocking him from running into the street or preventing him from hitting another child during an argument. And in the unlikely event that a child's actions pose a serious danger to herself or to others, we may need to temporarily use physical restraint—if this should occur with your child, we would notify you immediately.

Please feel free to discuss with us any concerns you may have about your child. This includes anything you observe or your child reports that could indicate the possibility of abuse or any other problem issue. We want you to feel safe in knowing that there are steps to take when problems arise. Our job includes supporting your family so that your child is safe and receives the best possible care.

Touch is vital to a child's overall development and we feel good about including it in our program. We want you to feel good about it, too. Again, if you ever have questions about our use of touch or any of our other policies, please feel free to discuss them with one of our staff members. We also have a Family Questionnaire for you to complete to help us understand how your child experiences touch. We hope you will complete it and return it to us so we can ensure that our contact with your child is appropriate and supportive.

Thank you for entrusting your child to our care. We will continue to do all we can to keep that trust.

Sincerely,

Supporting children's sexuality development

Dear Family Members,

Many parents and caregivers wonder about what is typical regarding children's sexual development. Children explore their bodies, including their sex organs, even before they are born. Sexual play and experimentation are normal activities and indicate healthy child development. Healthy sexuality development begins in early childhood and remains important throughout life.

Sexuality development in the early years unfolds in three stages. In the first stage, infants discover physical sensations and find pleasure in touching their own bodies; for example, they enjoy putting their toes in their mouths. In the second stage, preschool children continue to touch their bodies for self-soothing and for pleasure. Children in this stage may also touch your body, which you may find uncomfortable. Discuss with your child the types of touch you prefer. In the last stage, children may begin to use slang words for their body parts, they may be interested in pregnancy and childbirth, and they may masturbate at home and at school. During all three stages, remember that your child's learning is based on having experiences, and his or her sexuality development is no different. Be supportive by using appropriate names for body parts and by avoiding shaming your child for sexual curiosity.

Of course, this doesn't mean that adults shouldn't guide children's behavior. One particular concern of parents and caregivers is what to do if a child touches his or her genitals in public. When this occurs there are several steps an adult can take: (1) make sure the child realizes what he or she is doing; (2) tell the child that while it may feel good, that kind of touching should be done in private; and (3) help him or her understand the difference between public and private places.

For more information on this subject, you may want to read the books *Healthy Sexuality Development: A Guide for Early Childhood Educators and Families* (available from the National Association for the Education of Young Children; 800-424-2460) and *Teaching Human Sexuality: A Guide for Parents and Other Caregivers* (available from the Child Welfare League of America; 202-638-2952). We also offer a workshop to help families better understand their child's emerging sexuality development. We hope you will join us the next time this workshop is available.

Sincerely,

Family questionnaire

Please take a moment to answer these questions about how your child experiences touch. This will help us to better relate to your child while he or she is in our care. Thank you.

Child's Name _____ **Age**_____

Please check all that apply:

___ Your child gives hugs often

___ Your child receives hugs often

___ Your child rarely hugs

___ Your child likes to be hugged by family members only

___ Your child often pulls away when you try to hug him/her

___ Your child can't get enough touch—you cuddle all the time

___ Your child accepts touch, but needs to get used to the person first

___ Your child has had negative physical experiences
        (for example, burns or injuries due to fights or physical aggression)

Does your child's culture/religion have considerations regarding touch and physical contact? (An example might be restrictions between genders or between people who are not family members, or it might be improper or disrespectful to touch certain body parts.) If so, please describe those considerations:

_____
_____
_____
_____
_____

Is there anything else you want us to know about your child that can help us make sure any touch used in our program is respectful and beneficial? If so, please explain:

_____
_____
_____
_____

Sample Outlines for Staff and Family Training Sessions

After reading this book, use the information you have learned to share your knowledge with others. Unless otherwise noted, the training workshop outlines below can be used with both staff and families. You may wish to combine individual sessions into a workshop or series of workshops. The suggested exercises are listed here at the end of each outline, but most are best used as icebreakers—i.e., for eliciting introductory information from participants.

Significance of touch in children's lives

Goal: To increase awareness of the vital role that touch plays in child development.

Objectives:

• To learn about how positive touch affects physical, social, emotional, and cognitive development in young children.

• To understand what factors affect how, when, and where children are touched.

• To discover ways to incorporate more positive touch in early childhood settings.

Key points:

• Positive touch leads to positive physical, social, emotional, and cognitive development in young children.

• Negative touch and a lack of touch can lead to negative physical, emotional, social, and cognitive outcomes in young children.

• Many factors—such as a child's age, gender, or culture—affect the physical contact a child receives in his or her early childhood settings.

• There are multiple ways to incorporate positive touch in early childhood settings in ways that are individually, culturally, and age/developmentally respectful and appropriate.

Reflection questions:

• Think of a time when physical contact made you feel comforted or loved. What kind of touch was involved? What were your life circumstances at that time? Who administered the touch?

• Think of a time someone touched you and you felt uncomfortable or disturbed because of that touch. What kind of touch was it? What were your life circumstances at that time? Who administered the touch?

• Think of the ways you currently physically interact with young children in your work or at home.

Exercise:

Touch–Don't Touch. Place a life-sized cutout of a human body at the front of the training space. Give each participant one red and one green dot (pre-cut stickers work well). Ask participants to think about how comfortable they are with different body parts being touched by people they don't know: "Would a stranger get a handshake in greeting, while a friend might get a hug?" "Which parts of the body would you feel comfortable with someone you don't know touching?" Then, have participants stick their green dots on the cutout figure on places corresponding to comfortable body parts, and red dots on uncomfortable parts. Reflect during the training on how our personal comfort levels affect our contact with young children.

Suggested training resources:

Carlson, F.M. 2005. Significance of touch in young children's lives. *Young Children* 60 (4): 79–85.

Teaching children about appropriate touch

Goal: To provide a framework for helping young children learn the type and amount of physical contact each child finds appropriate and acceptable.

Objectives:

• To understand that what is appropriate for each child depends on his or her personal experiences and relationships.

• To realize that appropriate touch varies from child to child based on context.

• To learn how to teach body awareness to infants, toddlers, and preschoolers.

Key points:

• Children can participate in activities to help them discover their own body awareness and levels of body comfort.

• Children can learn the language they need to express their comfort levels to others.

• Without the above, children will have difficulty understanding inappropriate and abusive touch.

Reflection questions:

• What types of touches are appropriate from strangers? Why?

• What types of touches are appropriate from your friends? Why?

• When a child comes to you and hugs you, how do you respond? Why?

Exercise:

Personal Bubble (adapted from Adams & Fay 1981; Hart-Rossi 1984). Ask the participants to divide into pairs and have each person stand across the room from his or her partner. One partner slowly crosses the room toward the other partner, who is standing still. As soon as the partner standing still becomes uncomfortable, she or he says STOP! Have the partners switch roles, so everyone has a chance to try the exercise. Prompt the group to notice and discuss how the distances vary. A discussion of proxemics helps with this, too. Encourage each person to share his or her feelings regarding the level of personal comfort with varying degrees of closeness. Write the comments on a piece of chart paper and refer to them during the training when discussing how children's individual levels of comfort vary.

Suggested training resources:

Bailey, B. 2000. *I love you rituals.* Rev. ed. New York: HarperCollins.

Carlson, F.M. 2005. Significance of touch in young children's lives. *Young Children* 60 (4): 79–85.

Haynes, J. 2004. *Proxemics and U.S. culture.* Available online at www.everythingesl.net/ inservices/proxemics_elevator.php.

Tools for learning how, when, and where to touch

Goal: To provide adults with the tools they need to feel comfortable in providing children with positive touch.

Objectives:

• To learn about the body parts most children find vulnerable and about how to approach children when these body parts need to be touched for reasons of hygiene or safety.

• To become more aware of how culture affects touch preferences.

• To develop a "touch code" with children so they can learn to communicate their feelings about touch.

Key points:

• Children need opportunities to recognize their bodies' signals regarding what is comfortable or uncomfortable.

• Teachers and families can help children identify the difference between comfortable and uncomfortable touches, and help children communicate these feelings.

• Programs can involve families in the process of determining which touches are individually and culturally appropriate for their child(ren). (Tools such as the Family Questionnaire in **Appendix C** can be useful.)

Reflection questions:

• Think of the ways touch was and is used within your family and culture. Are there common types of physical interactions, as well as types of physical contact, that are prohibited? What are they?

• How do you communicate that you do not want to be touched? Do you use words; if so, what are they? Do you use body language; if so, what gestures?

• Think of a time when you welcomed a touch from one person but the same touch didn't feel as welcome when it came from someone else. What was your relationship with the first person? With the second person? What was the difference between the two relationships?

Exercise:

Cultural Comparisons. Prepare a sheet that offers a range of touch preferences typical of various cultures (using sources like the chart prepared by the University of Tennessee College of Medicine Chattanooga at www.utcomchatt.org/docs/erlanger%20culture-language%20guide%206-2005.pdf). Distribute the sheet, and ask participants to circle any of the characteristics that describe them. Have the group compare their responses, as a way to discuss cultural *and* individual touch preferences. (Substituting the Personal Bubble exercise would be another option.)

Suggested training resources:

Anderson, C. 2000, October/November. The touch continuum: Part of a risk-reduction curriculum. *SIECUS Report* 29 (1): 24–27. Available online at www.siecus.org/siecusreport/volume29/29-1.pdf.

Del Prete, T. 1998. Getting back in touch with students: Should we risk it? *Professional School Counseling* 1 (4): 62–65.

Hart-Rossi, J. 1984. *Protect your child from sexual abuse: A parent's guide.* Seattle, WA: Parenting Press.

Haynes, J. 2004. *Proxemics and U.S. culture.* Available online at www.everythingesl.net/inservices/proxemics_elevator.php.

Preventing, detecting, and reporting child abuse (for staff)

Goal: To develop an understanding of what factors lead to child abuse, what signs and symptoms indicate a child might have been abused, and what to do if suspicion of abuse exists.

Objectives:

• To learn about family risk factors that may lead to child abuse.

• To learn about the four types of child abuse (physical, psychological, sexual, neglect) and their accompanying symptoms.

• To learn the reporting protocol to follow when abuse is suspected.

Key points:

• Certain risk factors in families are associated with the occurrence of child abuse.

• Educators have a legal and ethical mandate to protect the children in their care by being aware of signs of abuse and reporting any suspicion they have that abuse has occurred.

• Educators also have a mandate to prevent abuse when possible by being aware of the risk factors and addressing them with families.

Reflection questions:

• Think of a time you suspected a child was the victim of abuse: What signs or symptoms caused you to suspect abuse? What did you do?

• Name three behaviors or actions of children that make you angry. How do you handle this anger?

• Think of three behaviors or actions you model in your classroom that might help a parent at risk for child abuse to not be abusive. How could you share these with families?

Exercise:

Stress Relief. Ask each participant to list favorite stress relievers. Encourage each participant to share his or her techniques. Record the ideas on chart paper. Refer to these techniques during the training when discussing family stress as a risk factor for child abuse.

Suggested training resources:

Carlson, F.M. 2006. *Appendix A: Detecting and reporting child sexual abuse.* In *Essential touch: Meeting the needs of young children.* Washington, DC: NAEYC. [this volume]

NAEYC. 2003. *Building circles, breaking cycles: Preventing child abuse and neglect* (brochure). Washington, DC: Author. (Companion guide available online at www.naeyc.org/ece/supporting)

Office on Child Abuse and Neglect, Caliber Associates, & C. Crosson-Tower. 2003. *The role of educators in preventing and responding to child abuse and neglect.* Available online at www.childwelfare.gov/pubs/usermanuals/educator/index.cfm.

Videos:

Concept Media. 1998. *The vulnerable young child: Child maltreatment, Part I: Neglect and sexual abuse.* Irvine, CA: Author. 30 minutes.

Concept Media. 2000. *The vulnerable young child: Child maltreatment, Part II: Psychological and physical abuse.* Irvine, CA: Author. 26 minutes.

Positive discipline (for families)

Goal: To learn about positive discipline, as well as what factors put families at risk for abusing their children.

Objectives:

• To learn about appropriate and effective vs. inappropriate and ineffective discipline techniques.

• To become aware of the risk factors linked with families who abuse their children.

• To participate in stress relief techniques for families and for children.

Key points:

• Any family is at risk of becoming abusive. There are certain risk factors that increase the likelihood that abuse will occur.

• Appropriate discipline techniques help children learn in a productive and nonthreatening way.

• Learning to manage your own stress is an important part of being a parent.

Reflection questions:

• Think of three behaviors in other adults that make you angry. How do you handle this anger?

• Think of three behaviors in children that make you angry. How do you handle this anger?

- Think of times you became upset, frustrated, or disappointed with yourself. How did you handle these feelings?

Exercise:

Stress Relief. Ask each participant to list favorite stress relievers. Encourage each participant to share his or her techniques. Record the ideas on chart paper.

Suggested training resources:

Cherry, C. 1981.*Think of something quiet*. Belmont, CA: Pitman Learning.
Cherry, C. 1985. *Parents, please don't sit on your kids: A parent's guide to nonpunitive discipline*. Belmont, CA: Pitman Books.
Child Welfare Information Gateway Web site: www.childwelfare.gov/index.cfm.
Gartrell, D. 2004. *The power of guidance: Teaching social-emotional skills in early childhood classrooms*. Clifton Park, NY: Thomson/Delmar Learning; Washington, DC: NAEYC.
Honig, A.S. 2000. *Love and learn: Positive guidance for young children* (brochure). Washington, DC: NAEYC.
NAEYC. 2003. *Building circles, breaking cycles—Preventing child abuse and neglect* (brochure). Washington, DC: NAEYC. (Companion guide available online at www.naeyc.org/ece/supporting)

Childhood sexuality development

Goal: To foster understanding of children's sexuality development and age-appropriate sexual play.

Objectives:

- To explain the stages of healthy sexuality development.

- To stress the importance of helping children learn and use accurate language when describing their body parts.

Key points:

• Healthy sexuality development in early childhood is necessary for optimum growth and development throughout life.

• Children explore and experiment with their bodies, including touching for pleasure; this experimentation is typical, normal, and part of healthy child development and behavior.

• Knowing what behaviors to look for during the stages of sexuality development can help parents and caregivers to respond more appropriately to children's actions.

Reflection questions:

• What are your feelings right now about discussing children's developing sexuality?

• Do you remember playing games such as Doctor or House as a child that sometimes involved examining your own or other children's bodies? What were some adult responses to such play, and how did these responses make you feel?

• How do you react when children play games that involve examining each other's bodies, or when they touch themselves at times that may not be appropriate?

Exercise:

Discussion with an Expert. To increase staff members' comfort levels with this subject, invite a knowledgeable expert to offer information and lead discussion as part of this training. Such professionals may include pediatricians, child psychologists, counselors, therapists, and social workers.

Suggested training resources:

Chrisman, K,. & D. Couchenour. 2002. *Healthy sexuality development: A guide for early childhood educators and families.* Washington, DC: NAEYC.

Chrisman, K., & D. Couchenour. 2004, March/April. Healthy sexuality development in young children. *Child Care Information Exchange,* 34–36.

Cyprian, J. 1998. *Teaching human sexuality: A guide for parents and other caregivers.* Washington, DC: Child Welfare League of America.

Honig, A.S. 2000, March/April. Sexuality and young children. *Child Care Information Exchange,* 27–29.

Honig, A.S. 2000. Psychosexual development in infants and young children: Implications for caregivers. *Young Children* 55 (5): 70–77.

Rothbaum, F., A. Grauer, & D. Rubin. 1997. Becoming sexual: Differences between child and adult sexuality. *Young Children* 52 (6): 22–28.

Video:

Learning Seed. 1998. *Raising sexually healthy children: Sexual development, sexual abuse prevention, and self-esteem for children under seven.* Lake Zurich, IL: Author. (Available from Magna Systems; www.magnasystemsvideos.com)

Infant massage

Goal: To encourage the use of infant massage by offering information on its importance and demonstrating relevant techniques.

Objectives:

• To learn about the benefits of infant massage.

• To learn about the research substantiating the importance of infant massage.

• To practice several infant massage techniques.

Key points:

• Infant massage is good for families: It is one of the best and easiest ways to facilitate parent-child attachment. It also can benefit immediate and extended family members, especially if any of these adults suffer from depression.

• Infant massage leads to a myriad of health benefits for the infant.

• You do not have to be a trained massage therapist to properly and adequately massage an infant.

Reflection questions:

• Think about the ways you now bond with the babies you care for—what are some of the things you do?

• What are some of the health concerns you have had or fear you may experience with babies? How have you treated these health concerns?

• Think about your own bedtime rituals—what are the things you do now to help you fall asleep and have a good night's sleep?

Exercise:

Think of Somewhere Quiet. Ask participants to close their eyes, imagine a quiet and peaceful place, and visualize themselves sitting comfortably in this quiet place. Ask them to breathe in slowly, hold their breath briefly, and then exhale slowly. Direct them to breathe in slowly again, hold briefly, and then exhale slowly. Next, ask participants to tense their foreheads and hold for a count of 5, then slowly release. Then ask them to tense their jaws and mouths and hold for a count of 5, then release slowly. Continue this process with shoulders, arms, and fists. Now, ask them to slowly open their eyes, and describe how they feel. Refer to these descriptions during the training when describing the benefits of infant massage.

Suggested training resources:

Field, T. 1993. *Infant massage.* Washington, DC: Zero to Three. Available online at www.zerotothree.org.

McClure, V. 2000. *Infant massage: A handbook for loving families.* New York: Bantam.

Video:

NurturingParenting.com. 1992. *Nurturing touch: Introduction to the art of infant massage.* Park City, UT: Family Development Resources.

Early years are learning years

Become a member of NAEYC, and help make them count!

Just as you help young children learn and grow, the National Association for the Education of Young Children—your professional organization—supports you in the work you love. NAEYC is the world's largest early childhood education organization, with a national network of local, state, and regional Affiliates. We are more than 100,000 members working together to bring high-quality early learning opportunities to all children from birth through age eight.

Since 1926, NAEYC has provided educational services and resources for people working with children, including:

• *Young Children*, the award-winning journal (six issues a year) for early childhood educators

• **Books, posters, brochures, and videos** to support your work with young children and families

• **The NAEYC Annual Conference**, which brings tens of thousands of people together from across the country and around the world to share their expertise and ideas on the education of young children

• **Insurance plans** for members and programs

• **A voluntary accreditation system** to help programs reach national standards for high-quality early childhood education

• **Young Children International** to promote global communication and information exchanges

• **www.naeyc.org**—a dynamic Web site with up-to-date information on all of our services and resources

To join NAEYC

To find a complete list of membership benefits and options or to join NAEYC online, visit **www.naeyc.org/membership.** Or you can mail this form to us.
(Membership must be for an individual, not a center or school.)

Name_____

Address _____

City_____ State_____ ZIP_____

E-mail _____

Phone (H)_____ (W)_____

❏ New member   ❏ Renewal ID # _____

Affiliate name/number _____

To determine your dues, you must visit **www.naeyc.org/membership** or call 800-424-2460, ext. 2002.

Indicate your payment option

❏ VISA   ❏ MasterCard   ❏ AmEx   ❏ Discover

Card # _____Exp. date _____

Cardholder's name_____

Signature _____

Note: By joining NAEYC you also become a member of your state and local Affiliates.

Send this form and payment to

NAEYC, PO Box 97156, Washington, DC 20090-7156